The Naughty List

The Naughty List welcomes you and
hope you will enjoy the following naughty calendar
filled with dirty jokes and naughty positions.

You will find a new dirty joke and sex position
on each day. Enjoy!

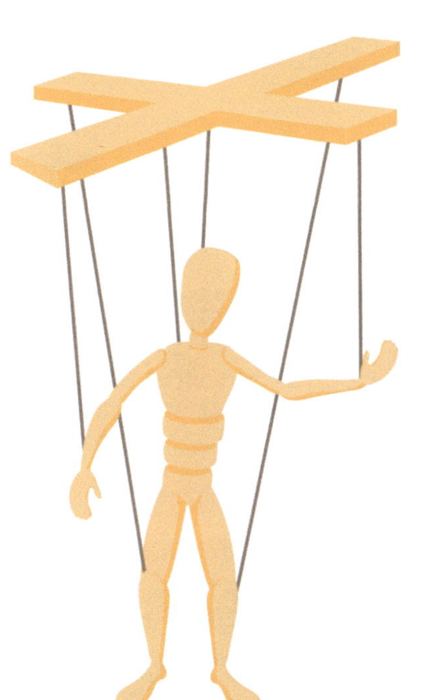

© Copyright 2022 The Naughty List - All rights reserved.
This document is geared towards providing exact and reliable information in regards to the topic and issue covered. The publication is sold with the idea that the publisher is not required to render accounting, officially permitted, or otherwise, qualified services. If advice is necessary, legal or professional, a practiced individual in the profession should be ordered.

- From a Declaration of Principles which was accepted and approved equally by a Committee of the American Bar Association and a Committee of Publishers and Associations.

In no way is it legal to reproduce, duplicate, or transmit any part of this document in either electronic means or in printed format. Recording of this publication is strictly prohibited and any storage of this document is not allowed unless with written permission from the publisher. All rights reserved.

The information provided herein is stated to be truthful and consistent, in that any liability, in terms of inattention or otherwise, by any usage or abuse of any policies, processes, or directions contained within is the solitary and utter responsibility of the recipient reader. Under no circumstances will any legal responsibility or blame be held against the publisher for any reparation, damages, or monetary loss due to the information herein, either directly or indirectly.

Respective authors own all copyrights not held by the publisher.
The information herein is offered for informational purposes solely, and is universal as so. The presentation of the information is without contract or any type of guarantee assurance.

The trademarks that are used are without any consent, and the publication of the trademark is without permission or backing by the trademark owner. All trademarks and brands within this book are for clarifying purposes only and are the owned by the owners themselves, not affiliated with this document.

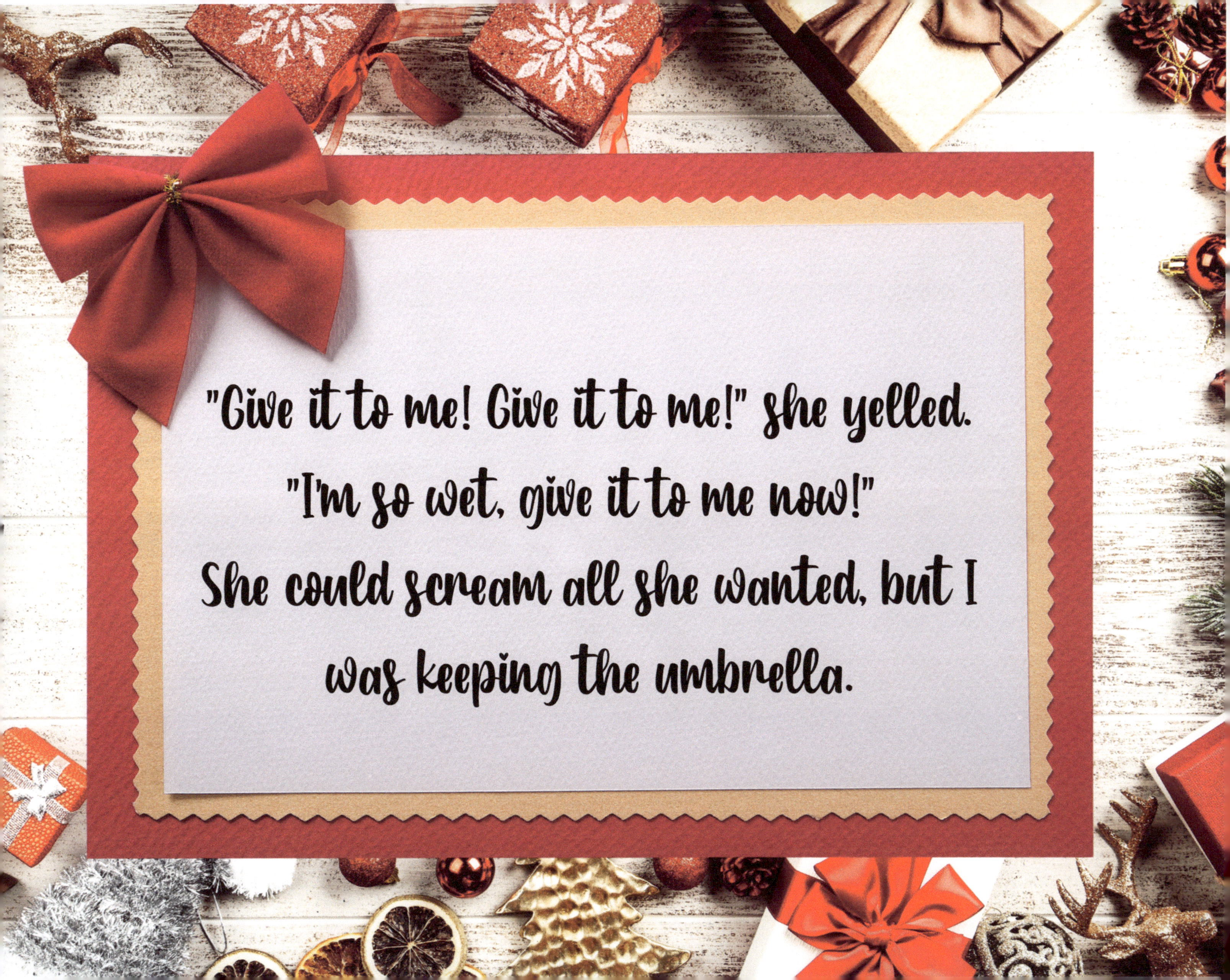

"Give it to me! Give it to me!" she yelled. "I'm so wet, give it to me now!" She could scream all she wanted, but I was keeping the umbrella.

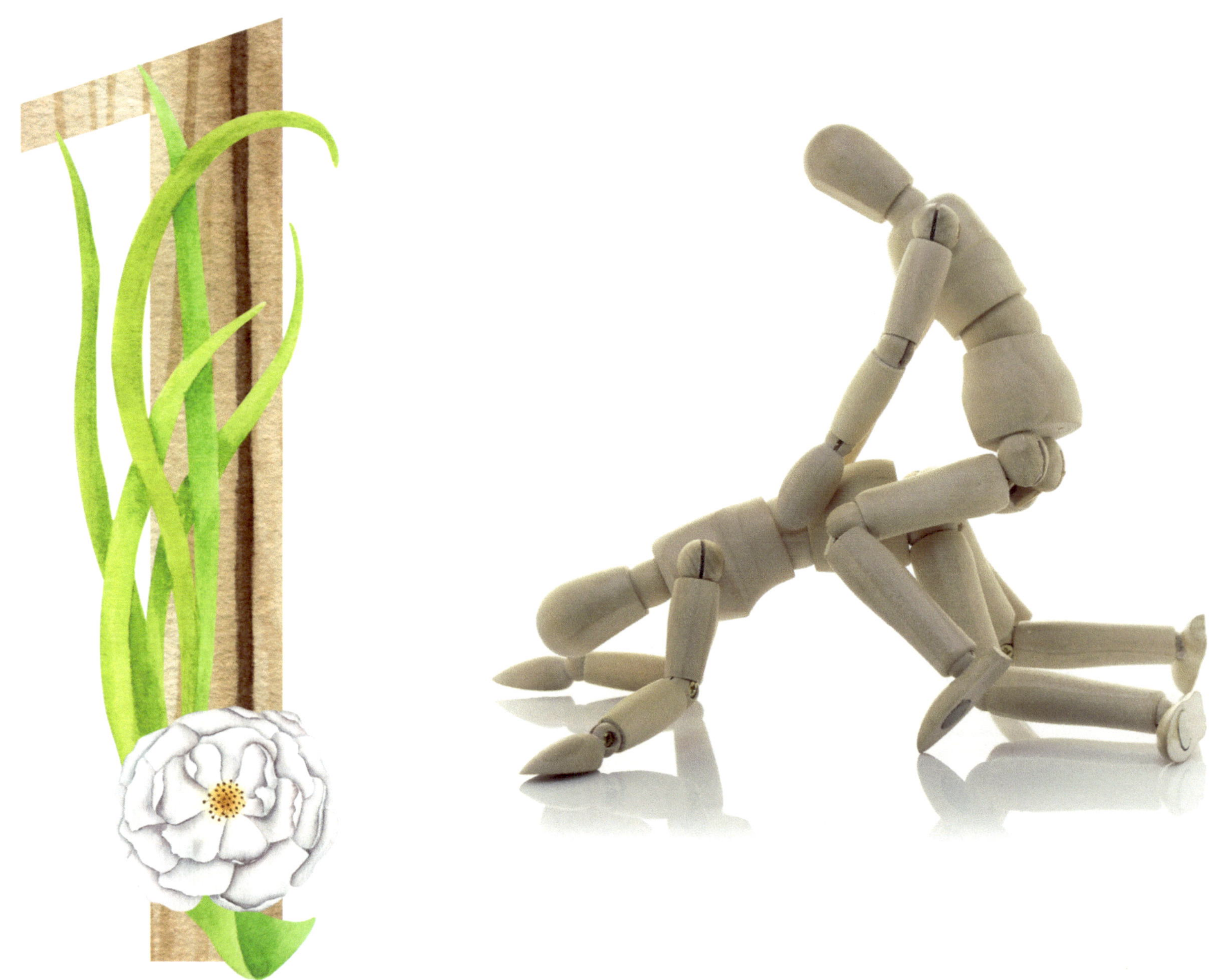

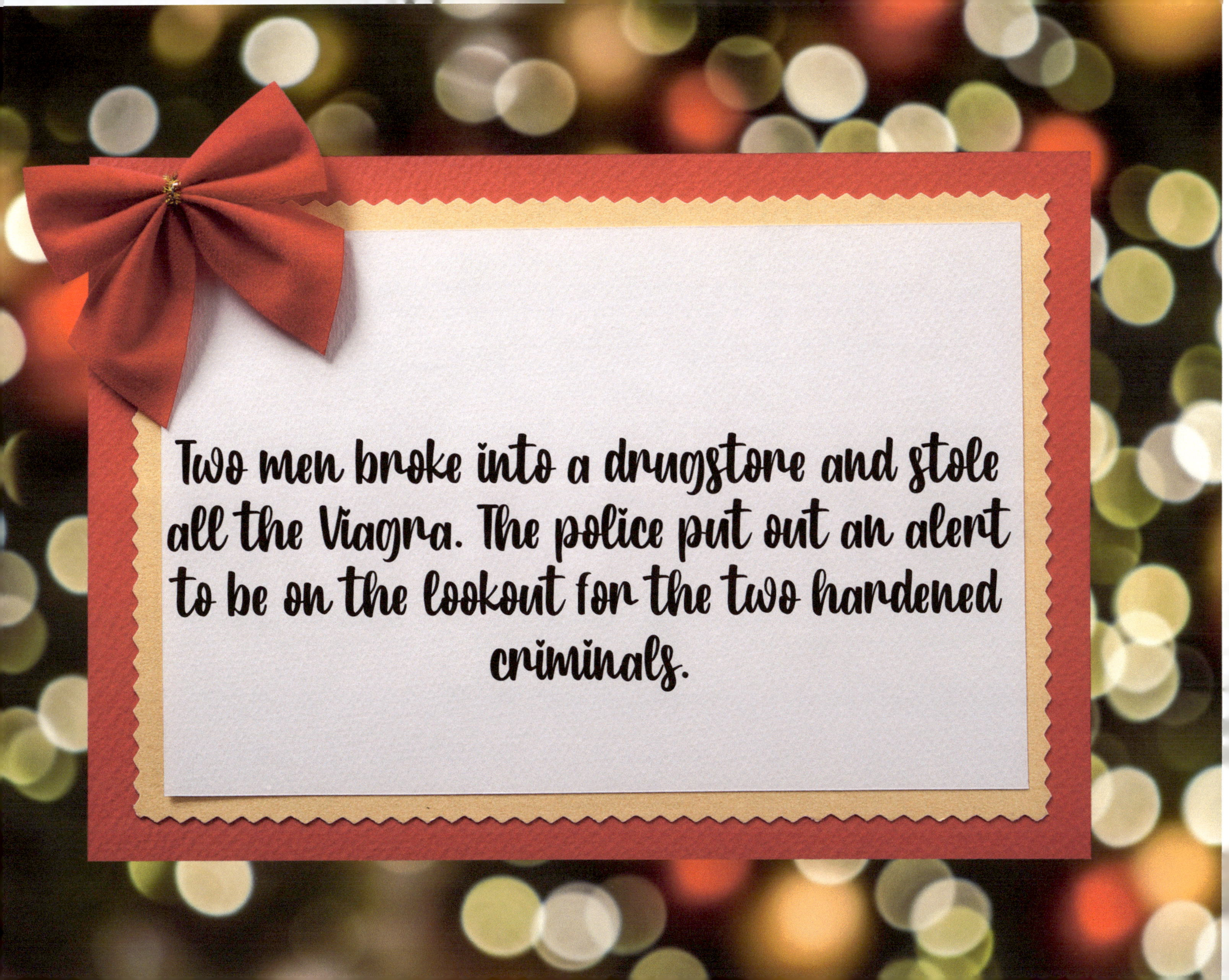
Two men broke into a drugstore and stole all the Viagra. The police put out an alert to be on the lookout for the two hardened criminals.

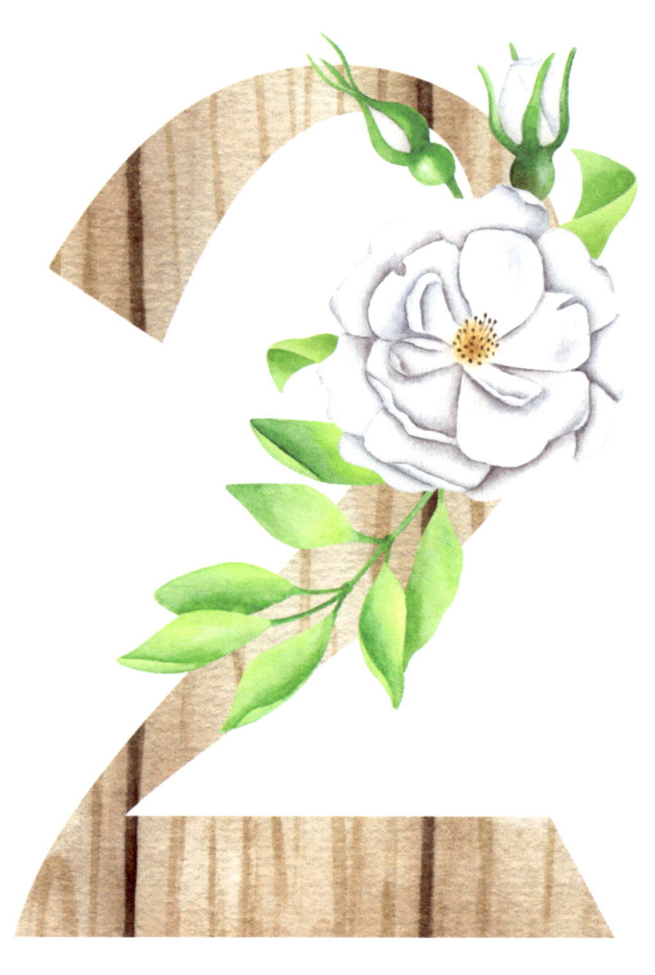

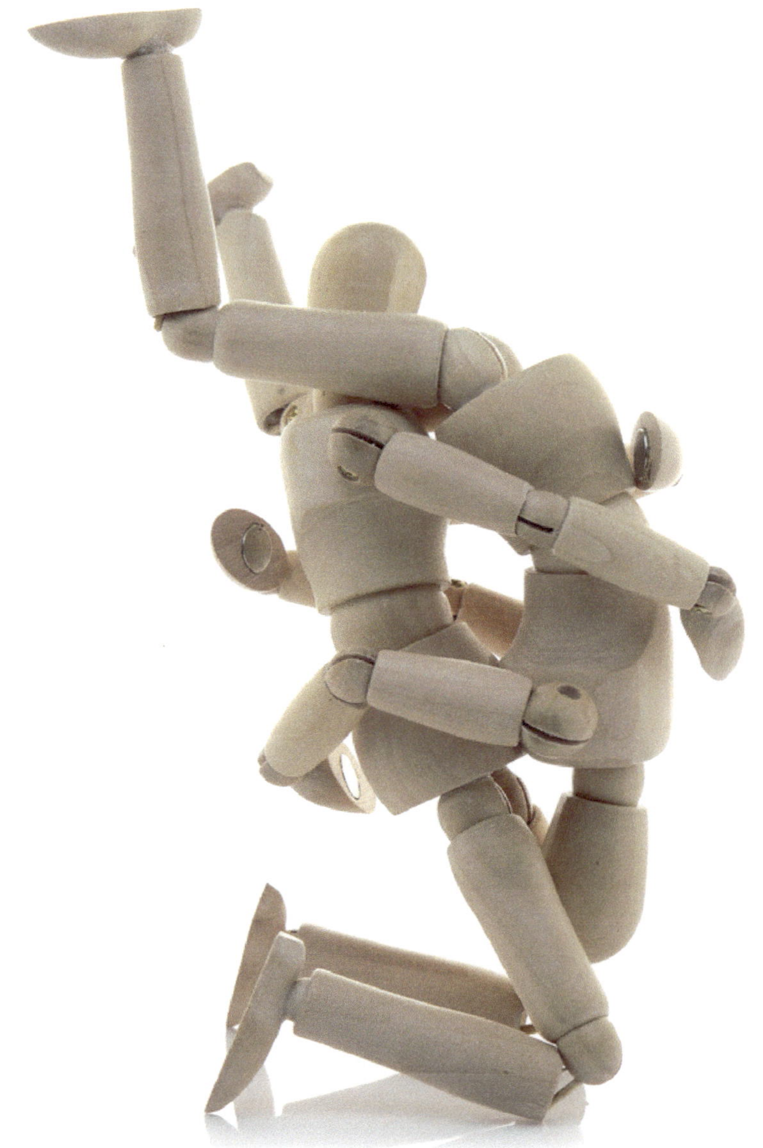

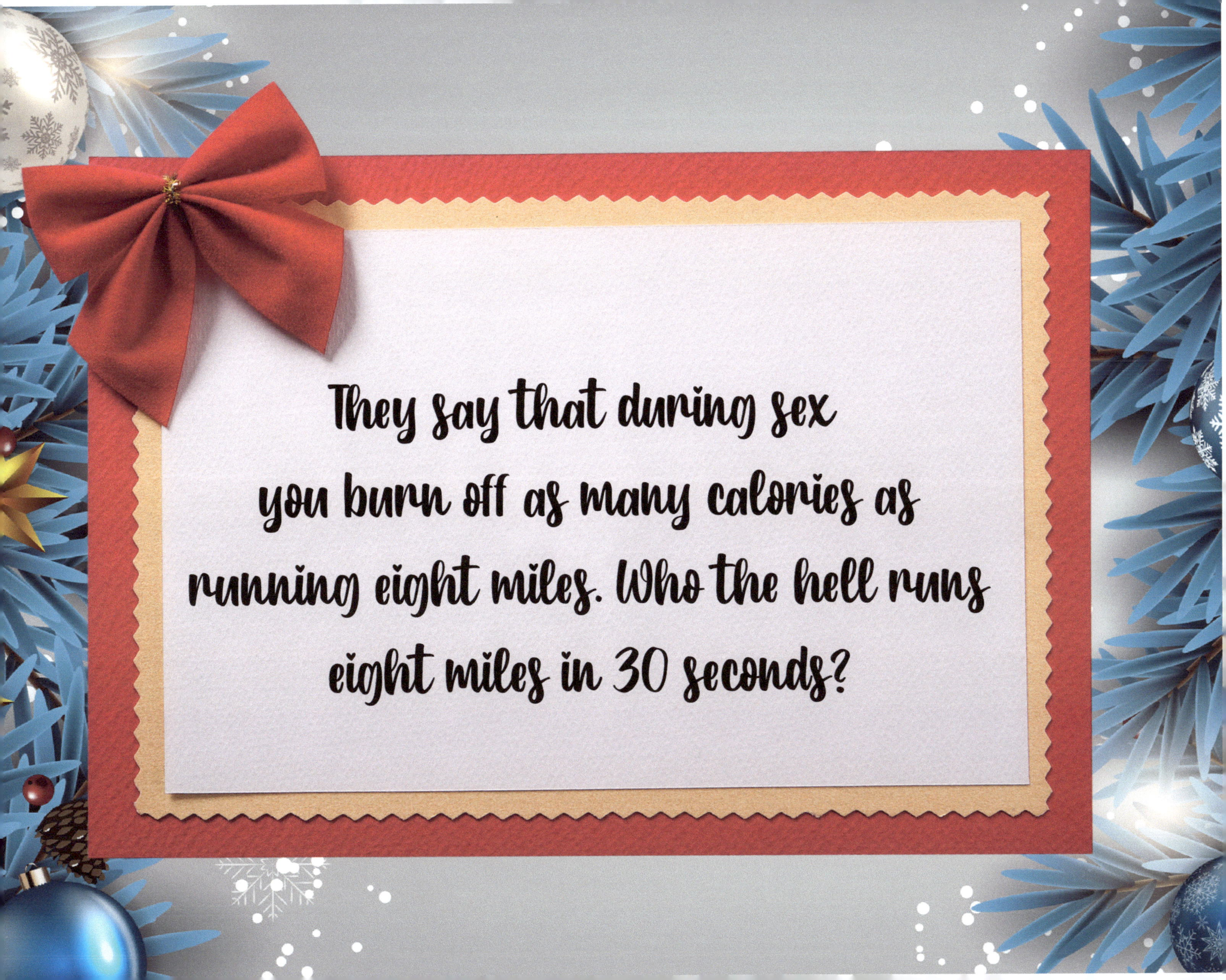
They say that during sex
you burn off as many calories as
running eight miles. Who the hell runs
eight miles in 30 seconds?

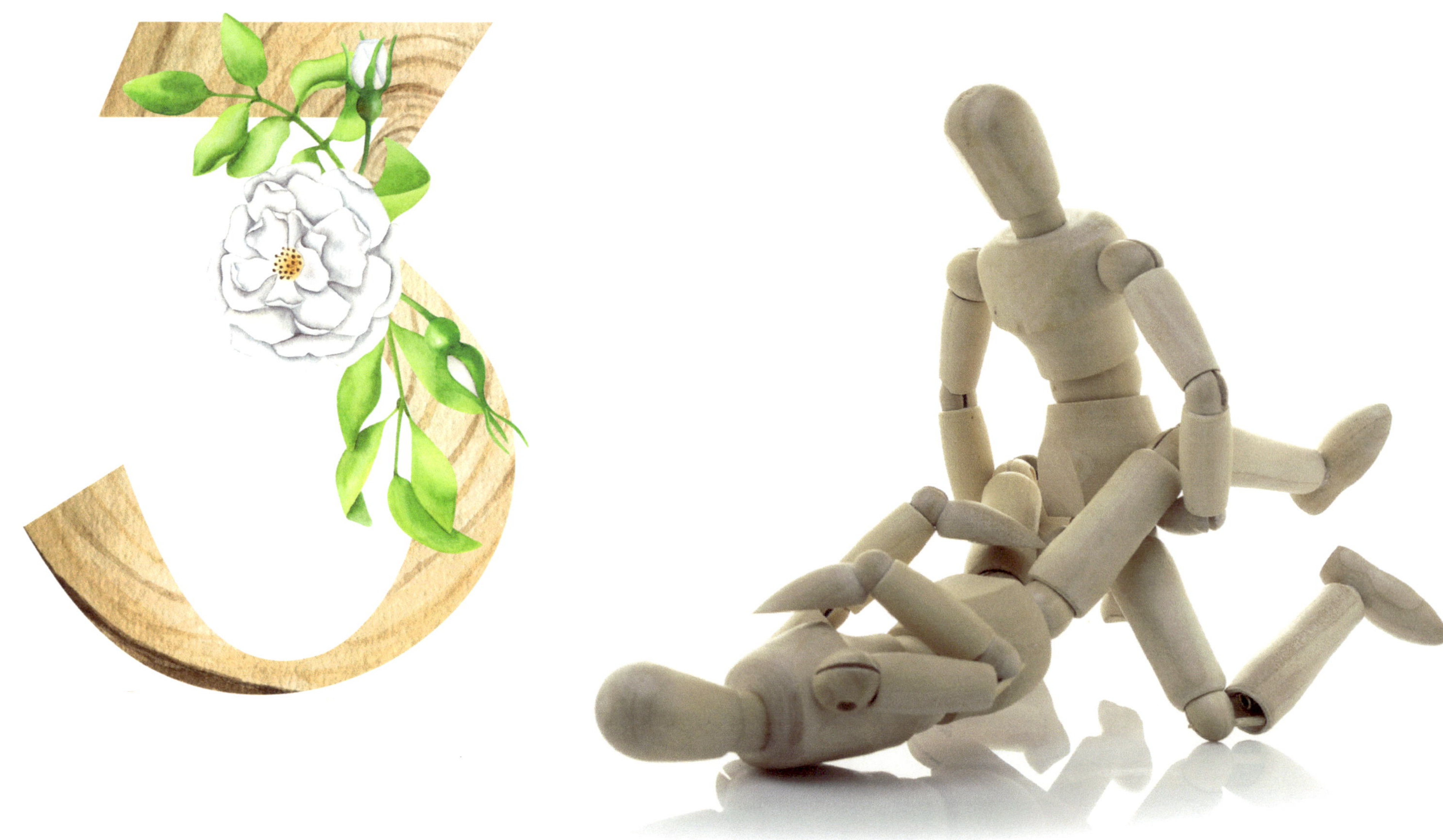

I'll admit it, I have a tremendous sex drive. My girlfriend lives forty miles away.

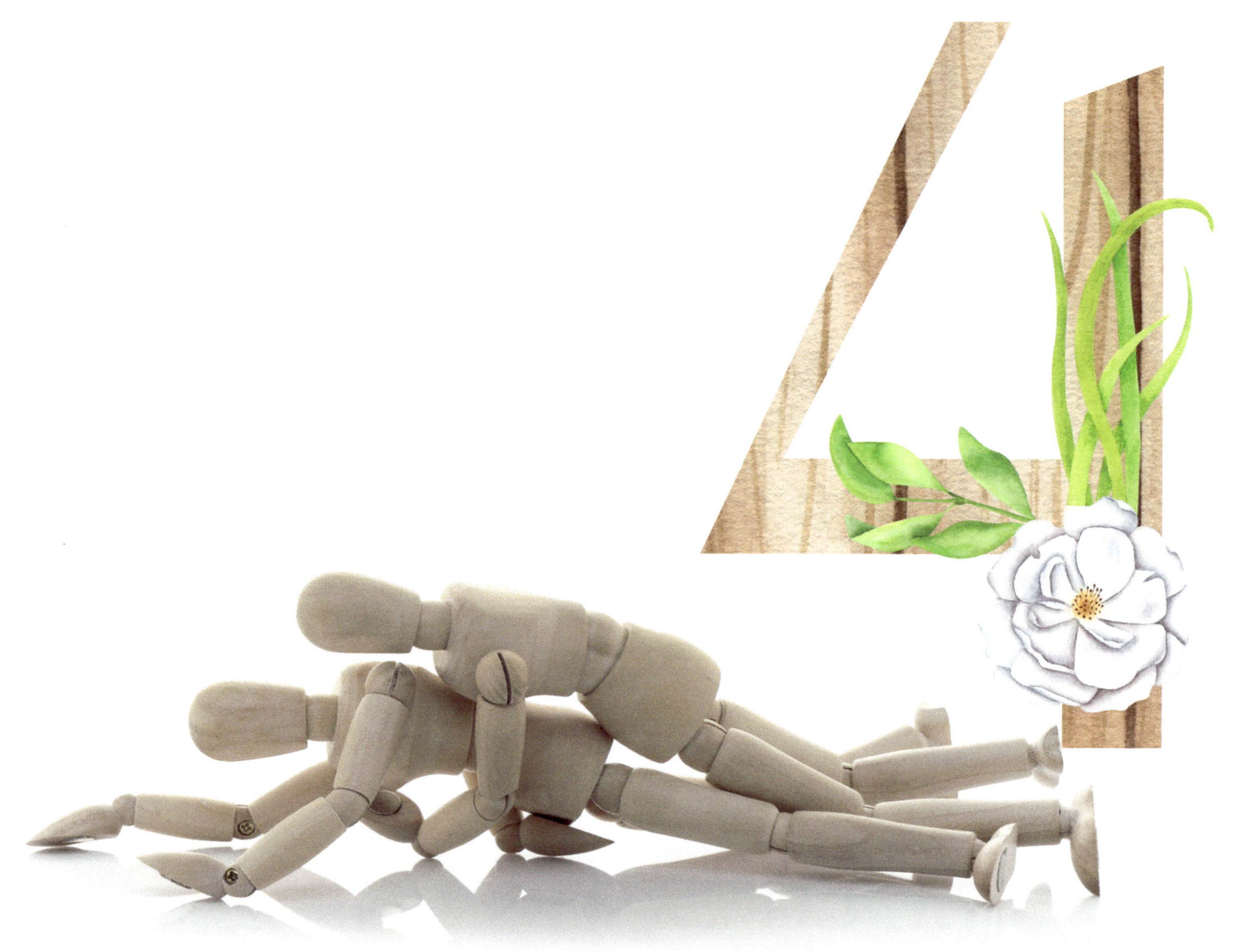

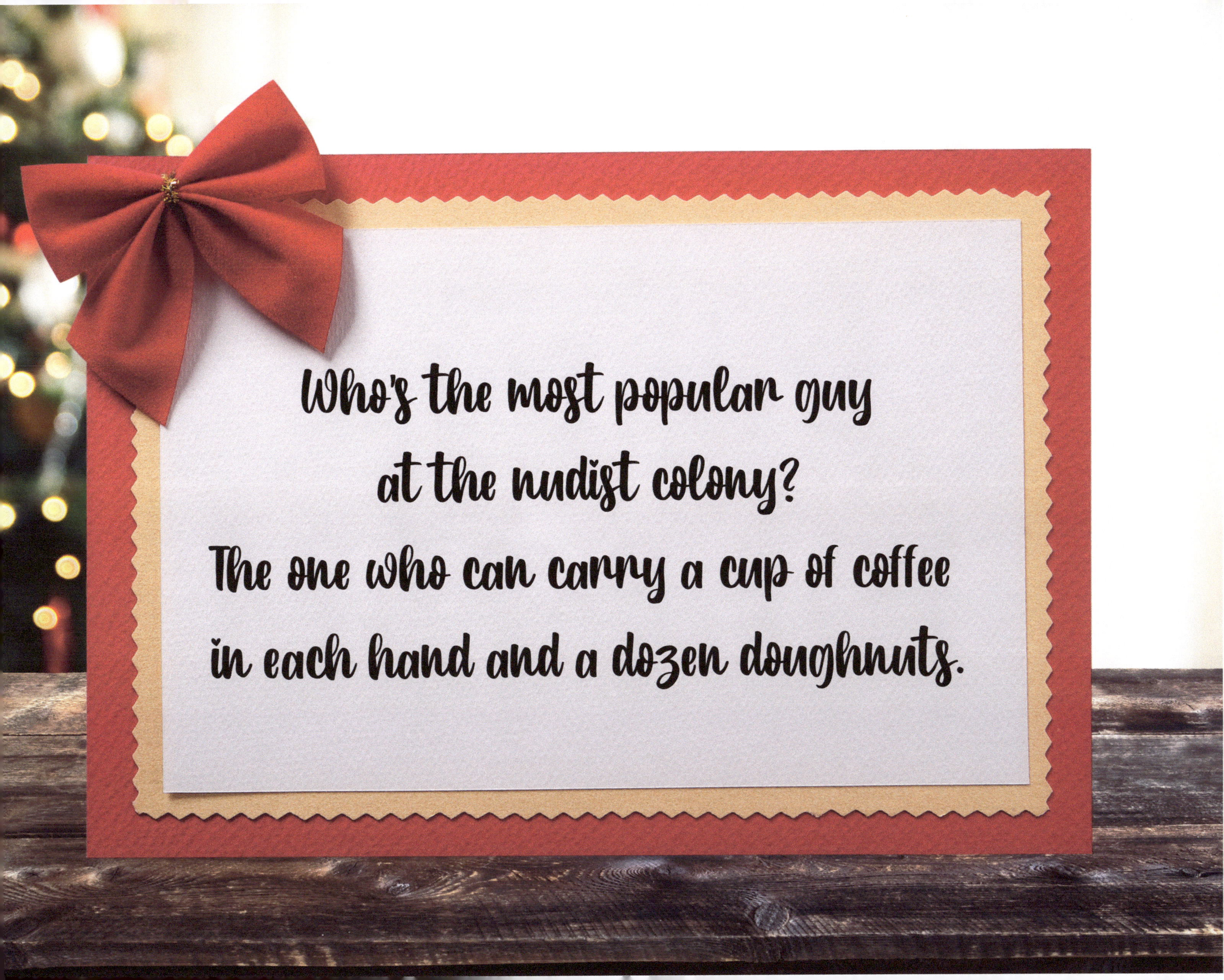
Who's the most popular guy
at the nudist colony?
The one who can carry a cup of coffee
in each hand and a dozen doughnuts.

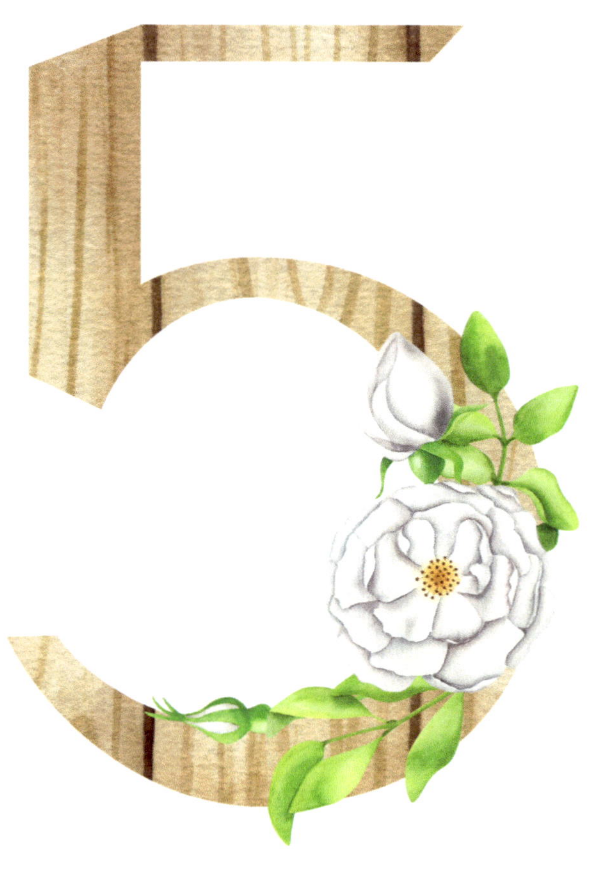

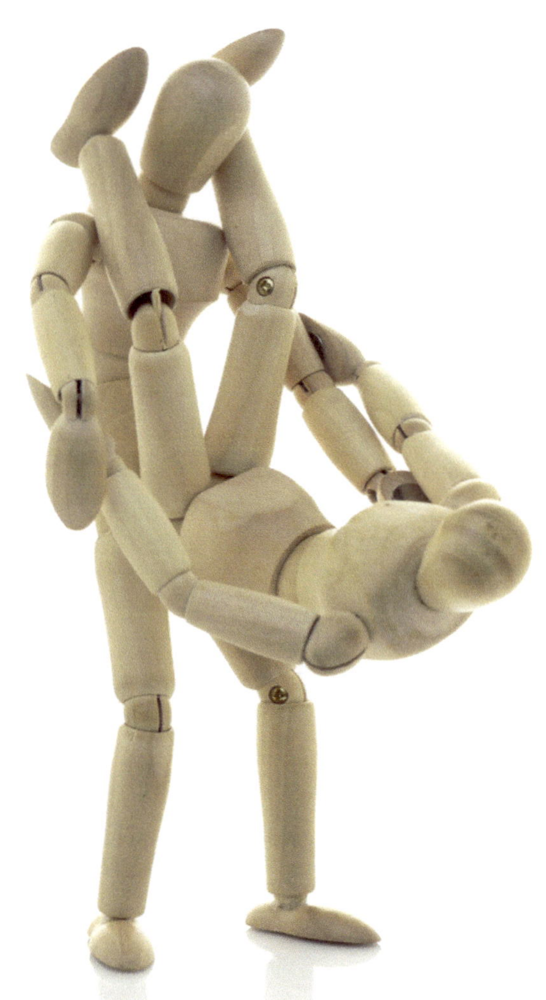

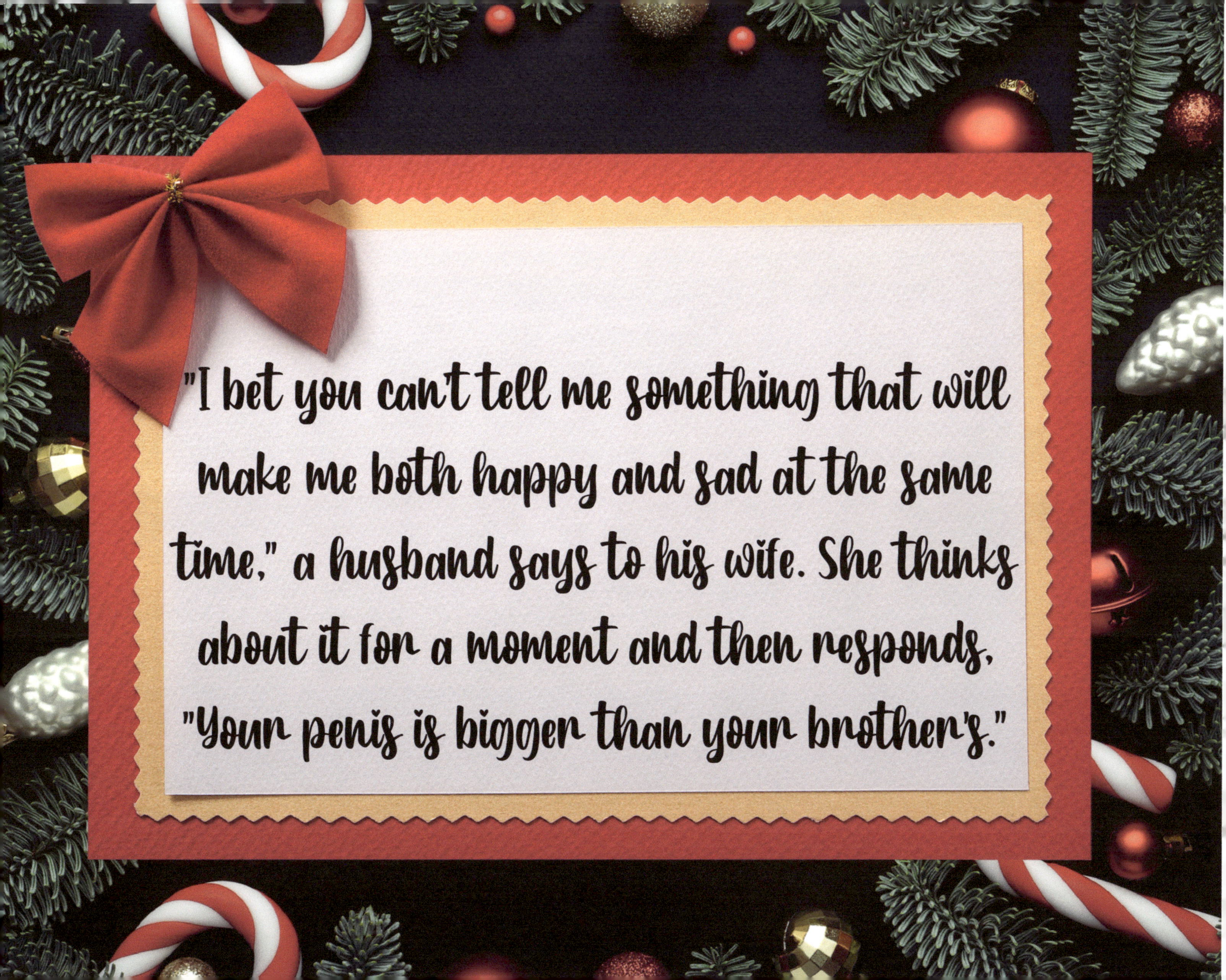
"I bet you can't tell me something that will make me both happy and sad at the same time," a husband says to his wife. She thinks about it for a moment and then responds, "Your penis is bigger than your brother's."

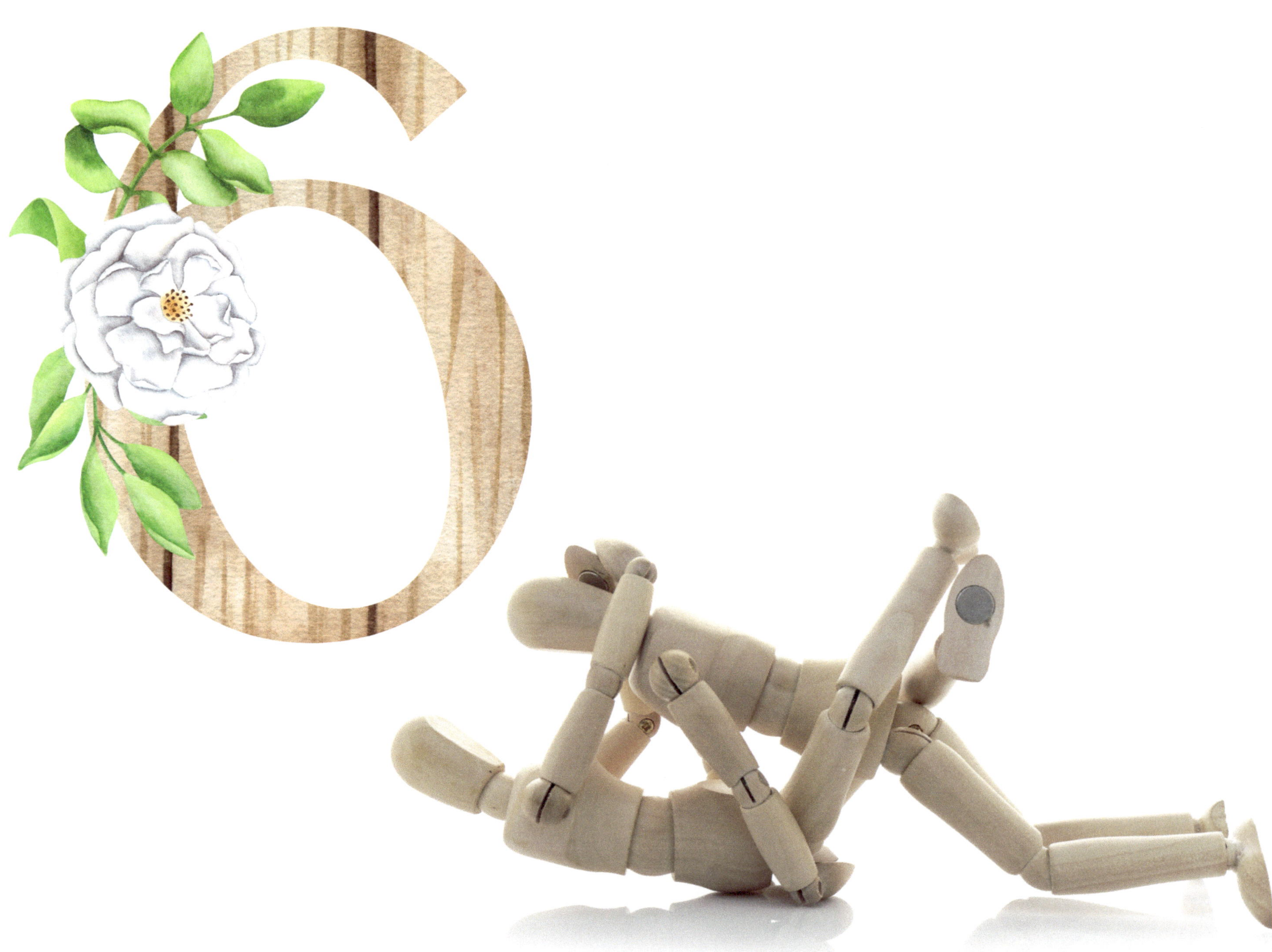

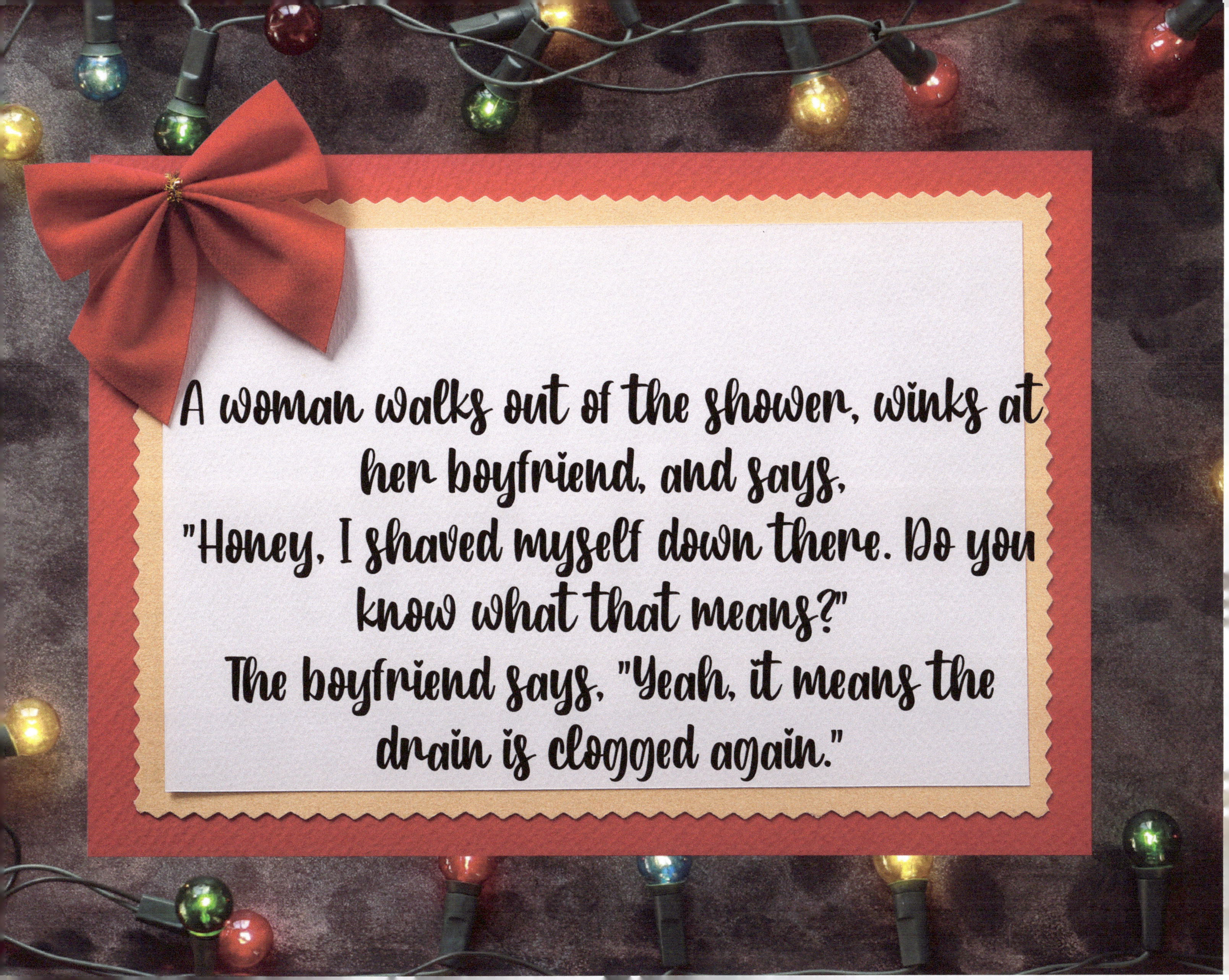
A woman walks out of the shower, winks at
her boyfriend, and says,
"Honey, I shaved myself down there. Do you
know what that means?"
The boyfriend says, "Yeah, it means the
drain is clogged again."

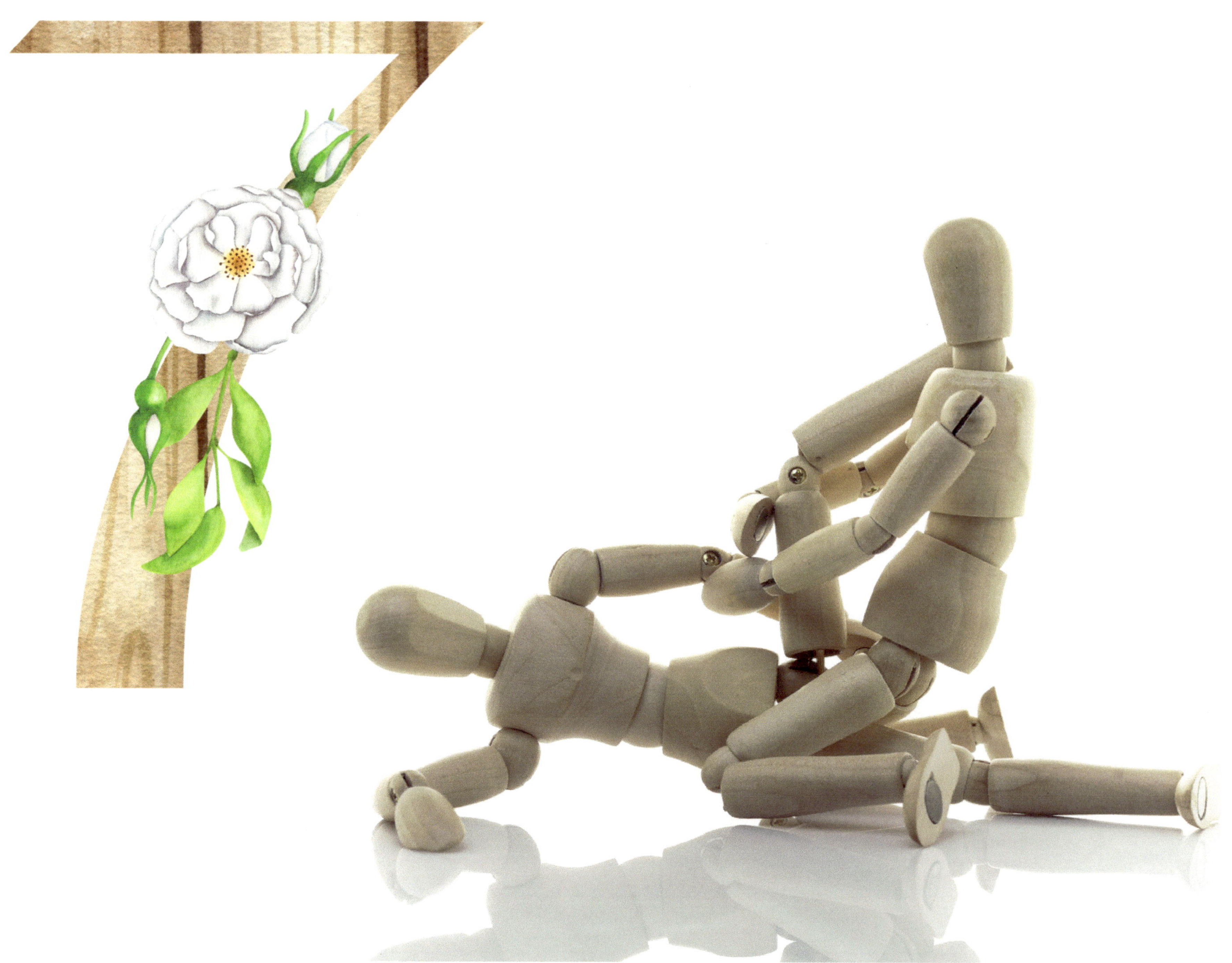
7

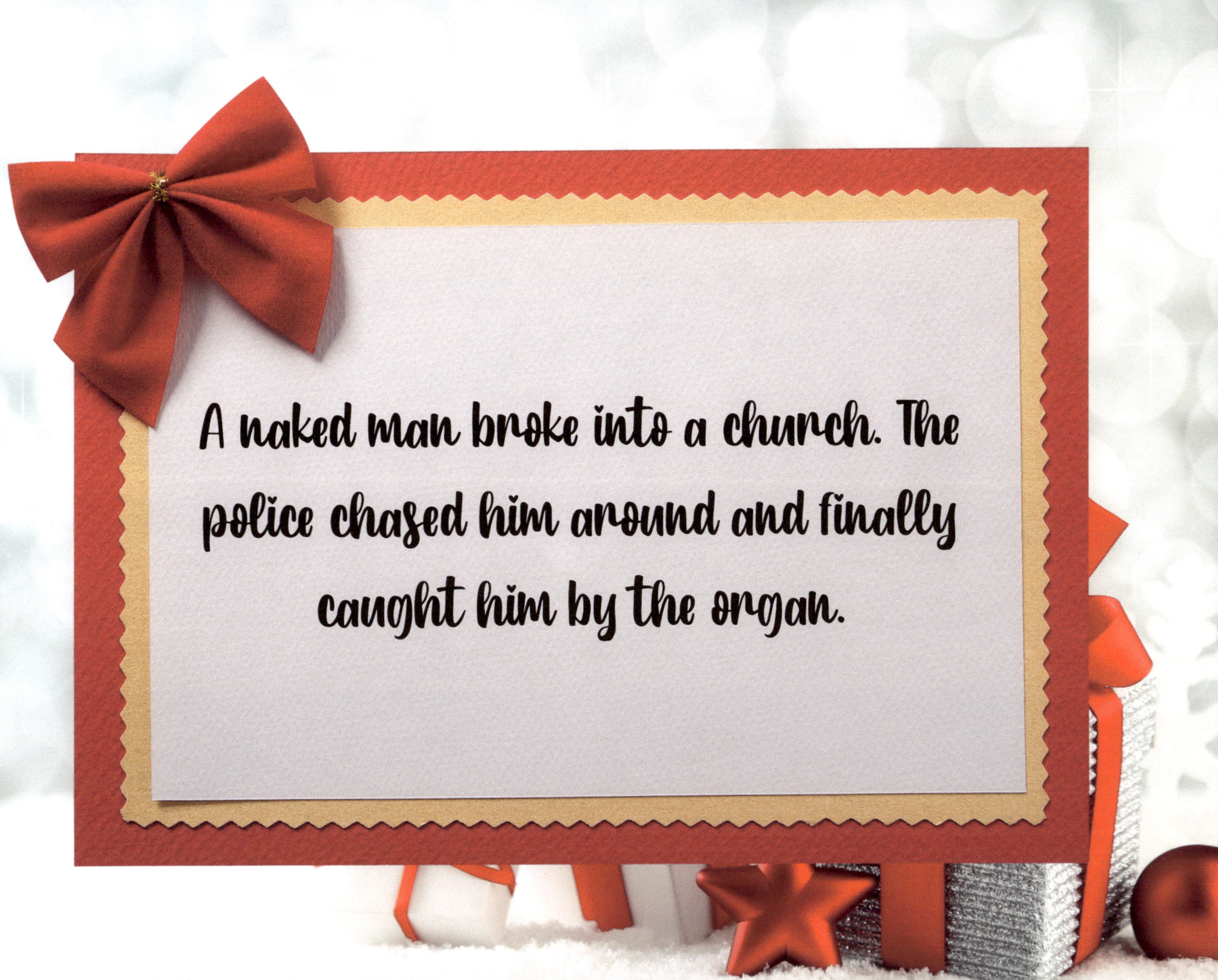
A naked man broke into a church. The police chased him around and finally caught him by the organ.

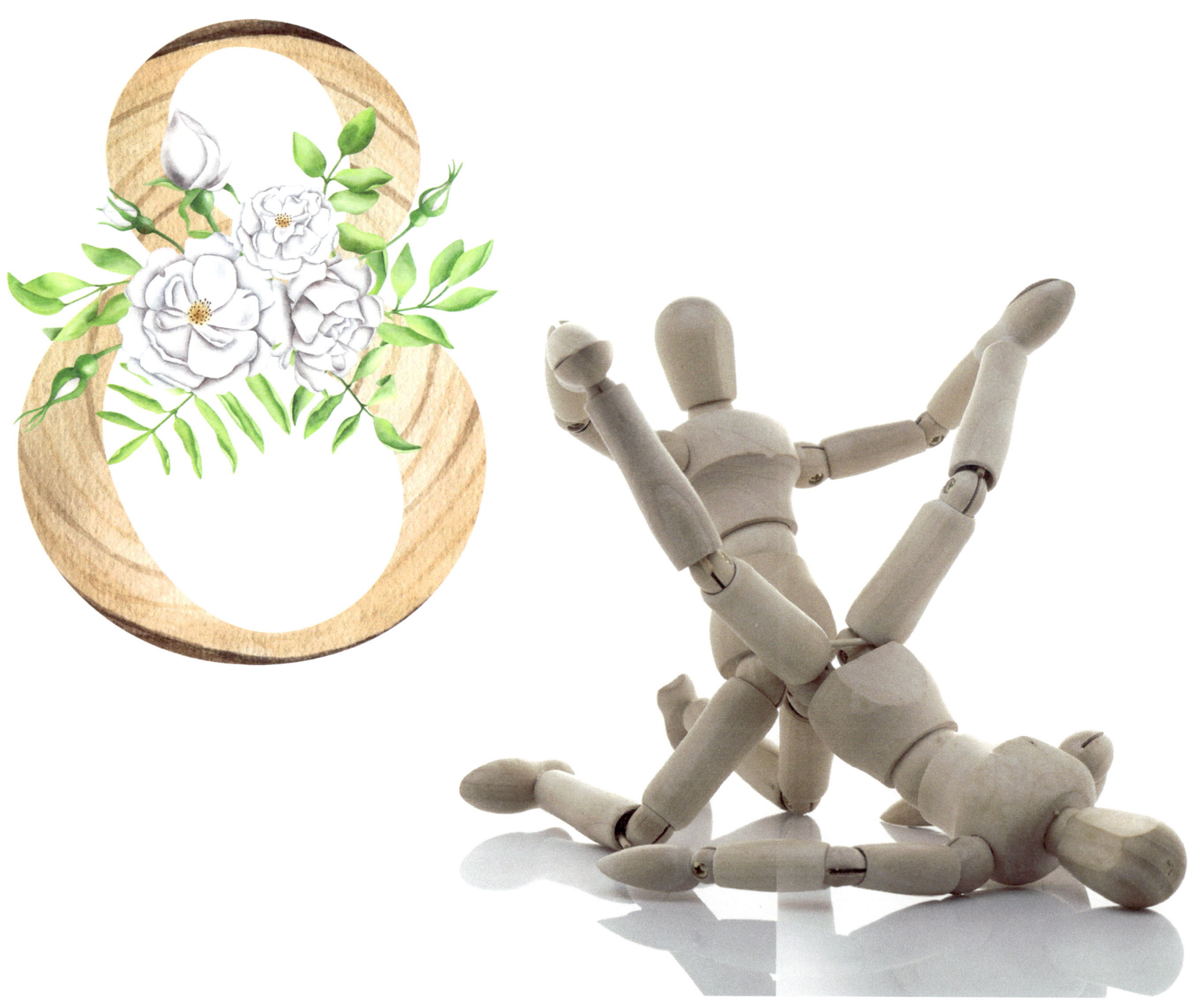

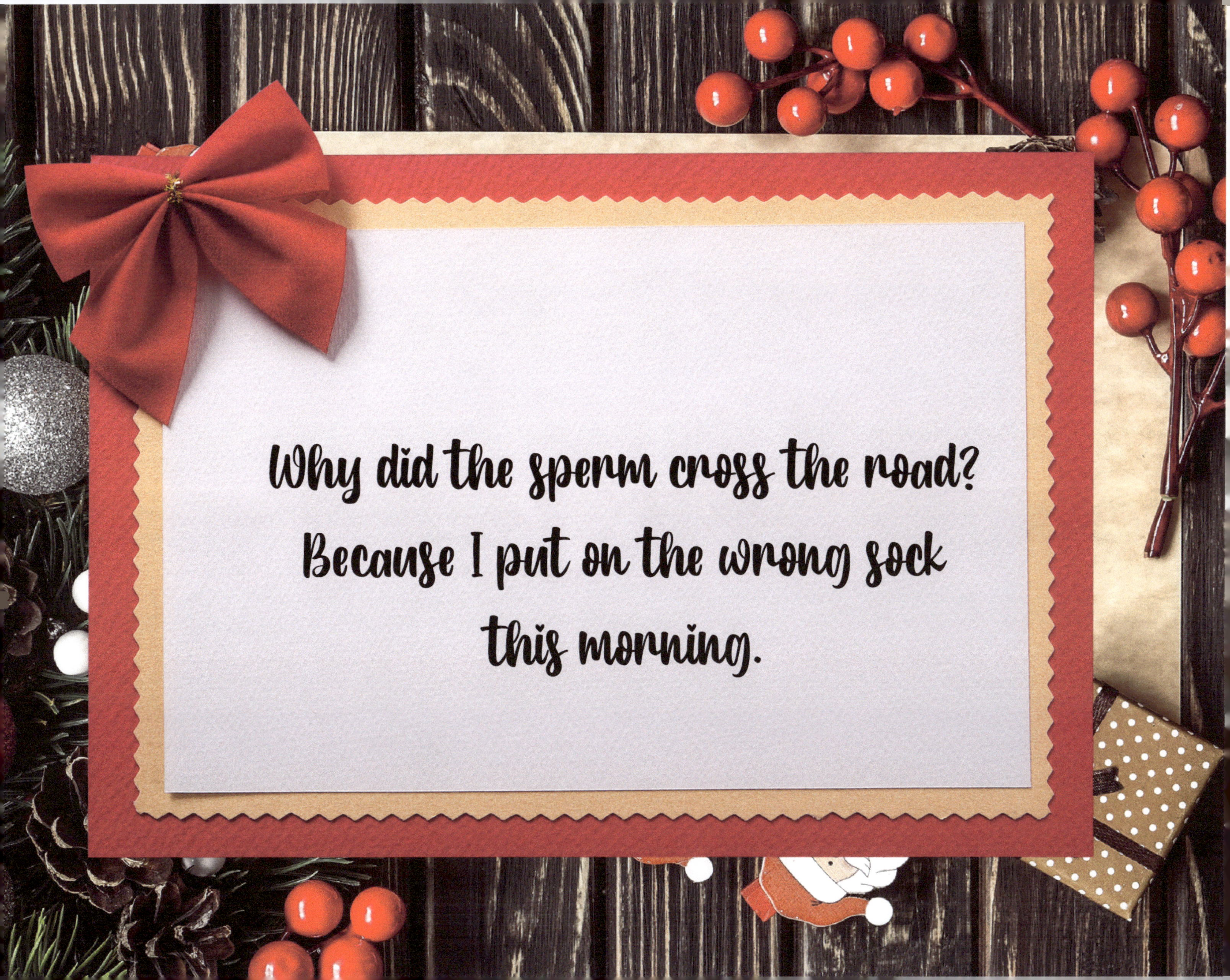
Why did the sperm cross the road?
Because I put on the wrong sock
this morning.

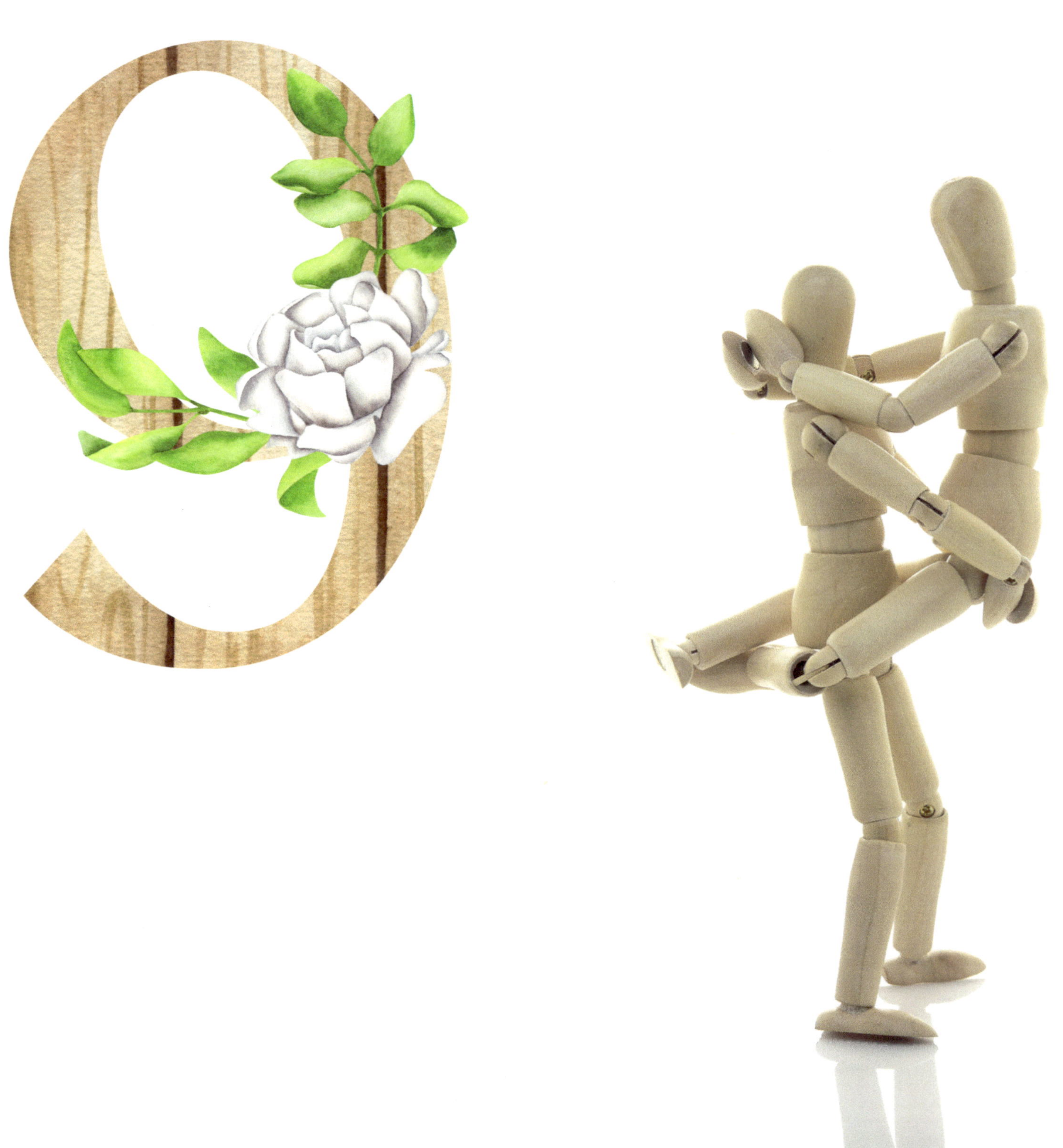
9

An old woman walked into a dentist's office, took off all her clothes, and spread her legs. The dentist said, "I think you have the wrong room." "You put in my husband's teeth last week," she replied. "Now you have to remove them."

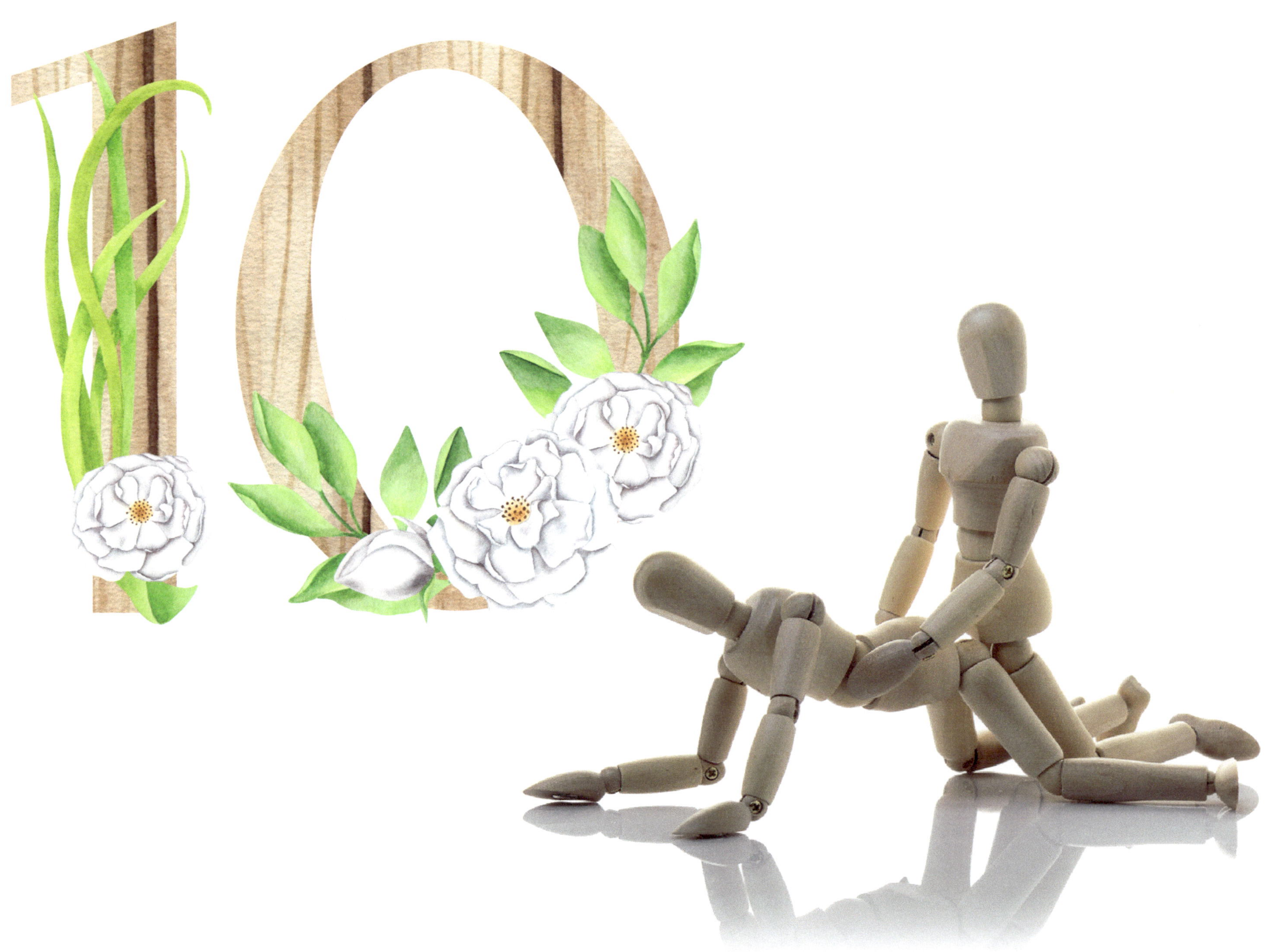

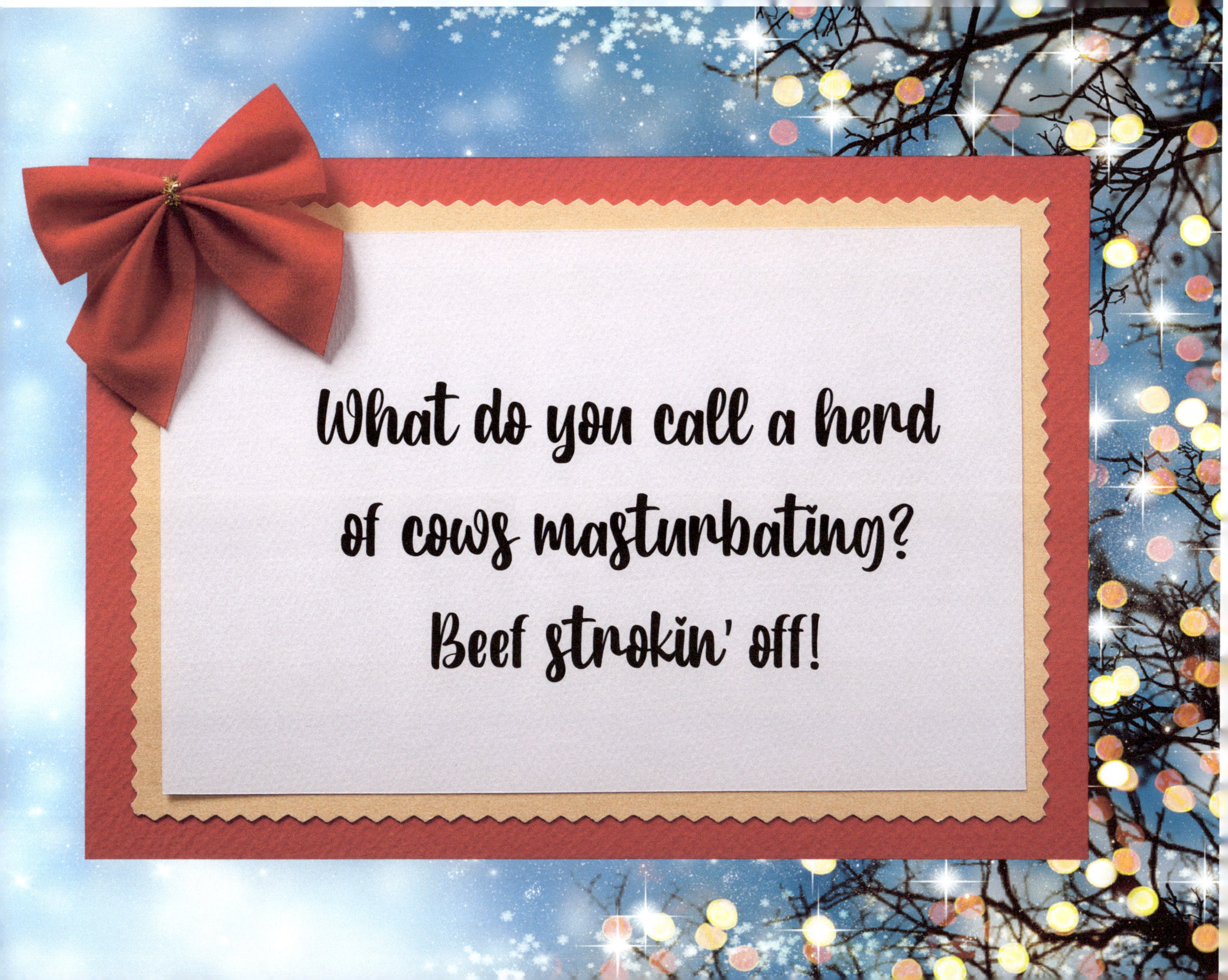
What do you call a herd
of cows masturbating?
Beef strokin' off!

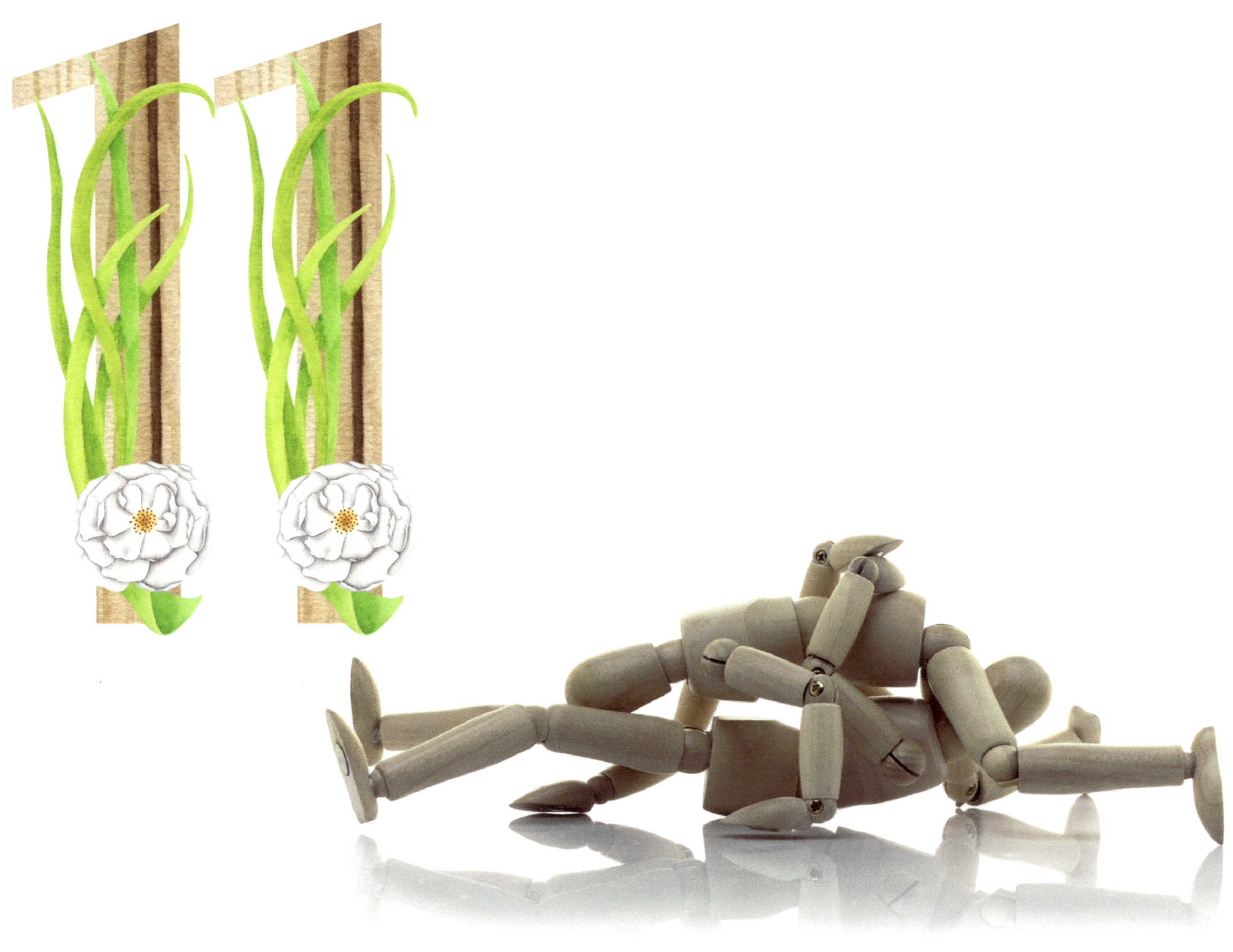

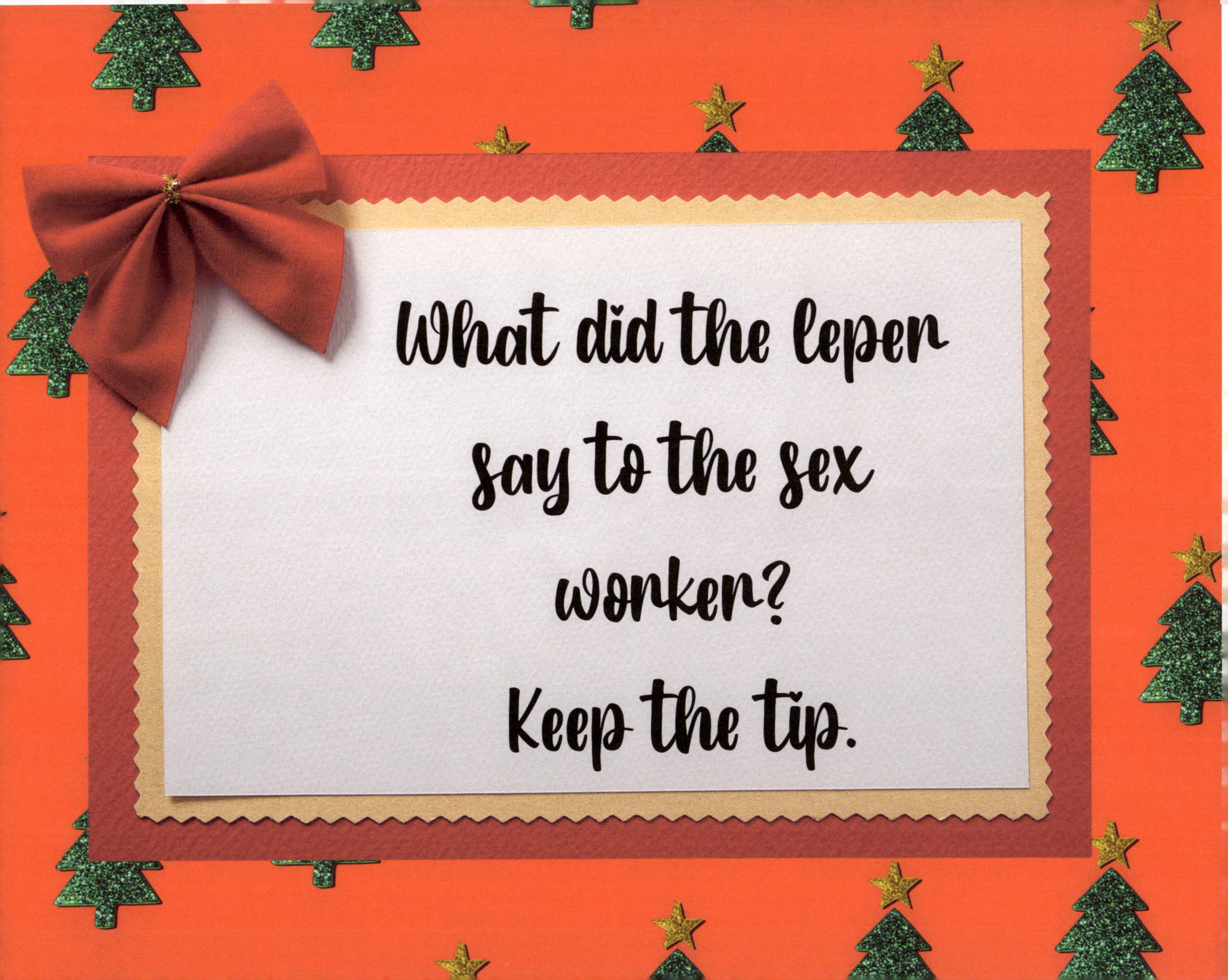
What did the leper
say to the sex
worker?
Keep the tip.

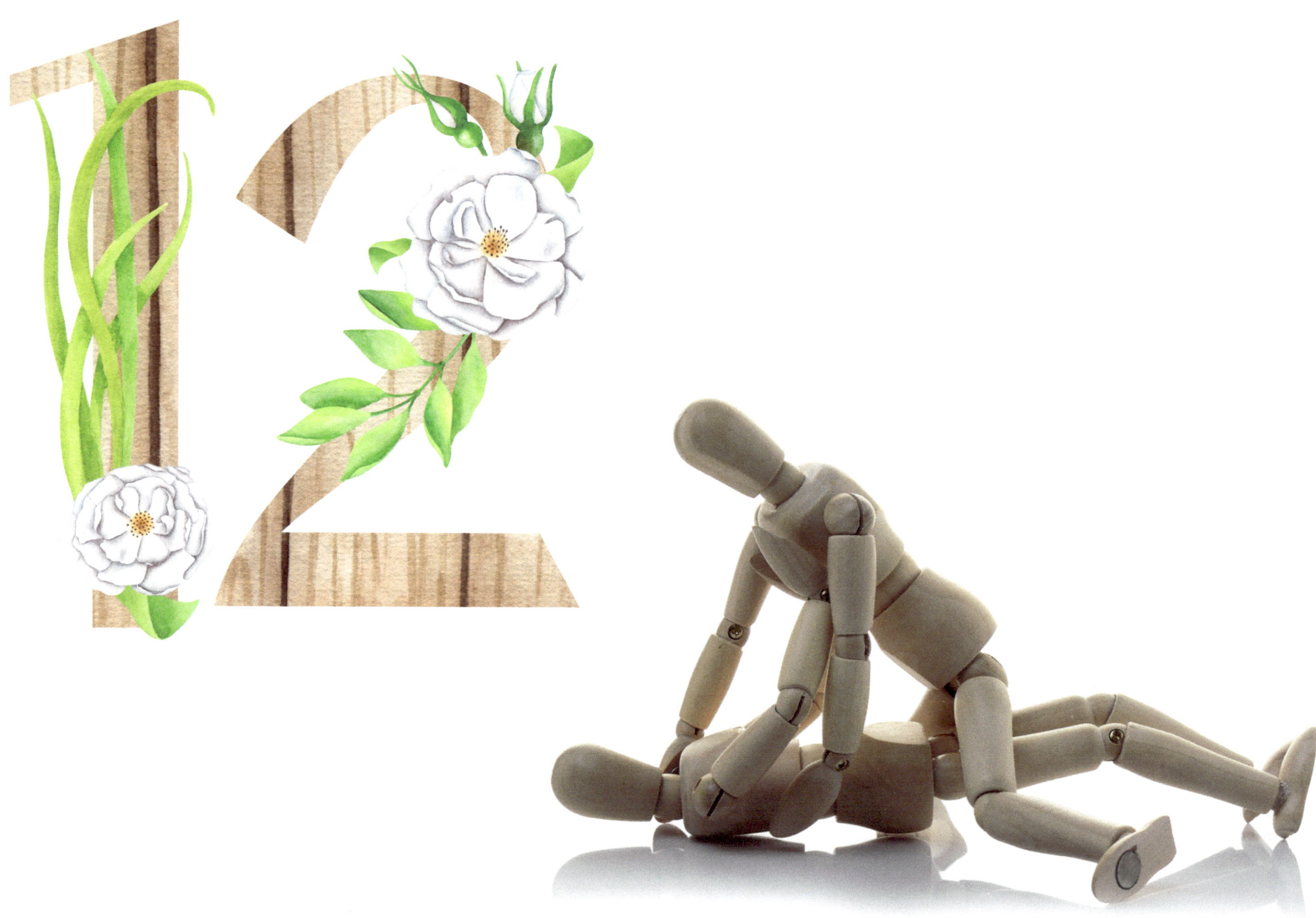
12

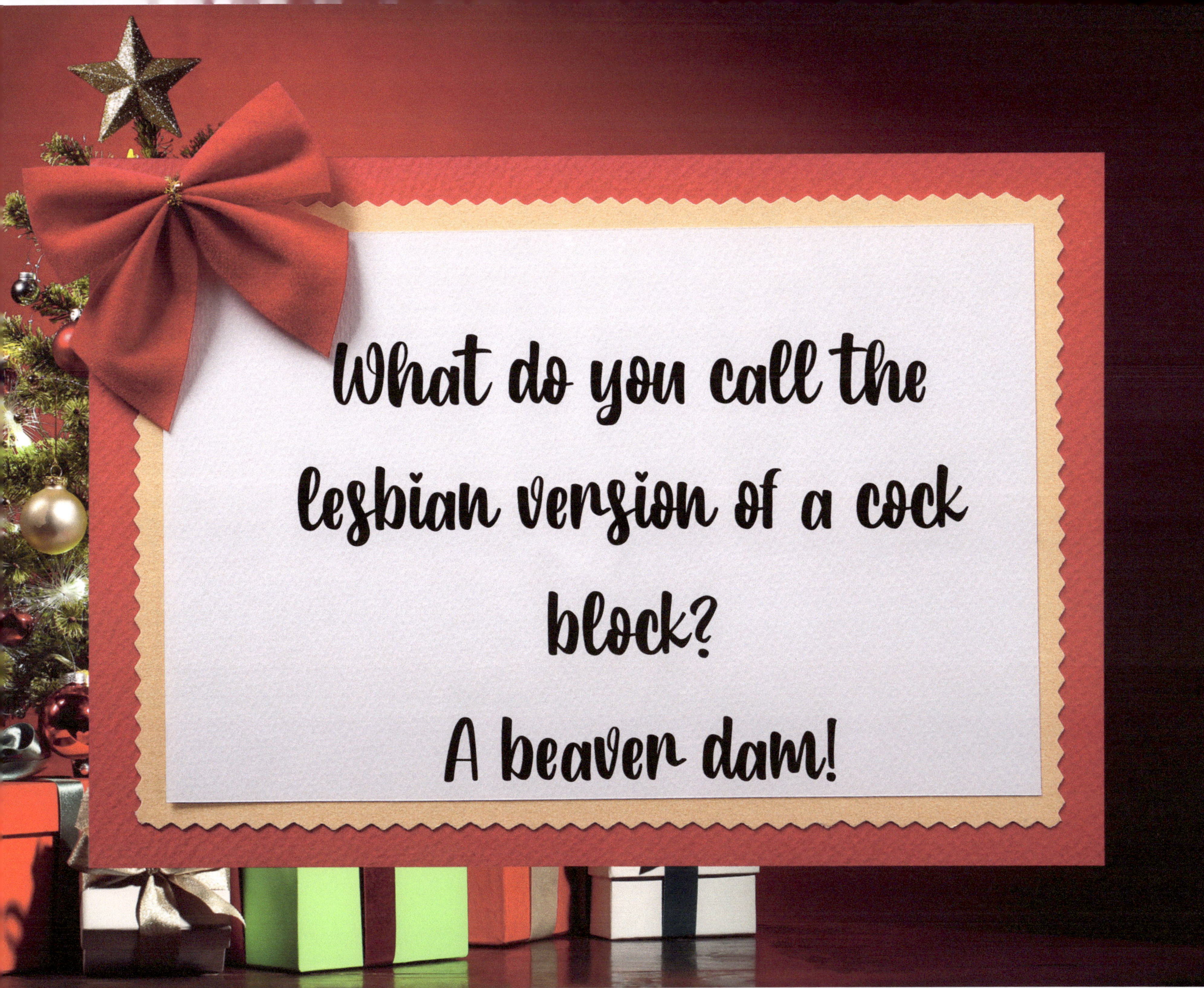
What do you call the
lesbian version of a cock
block?
A beaver dam!

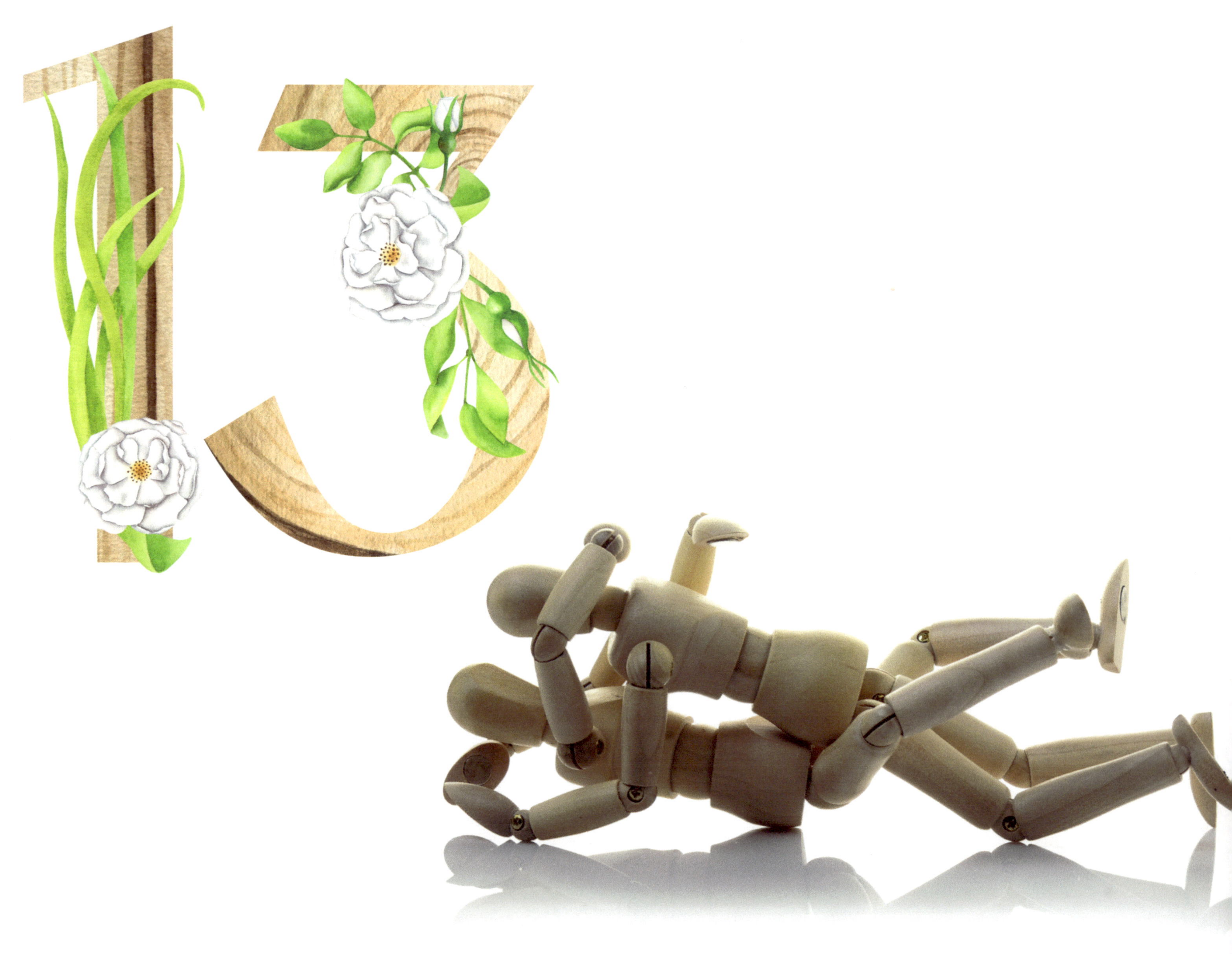
13

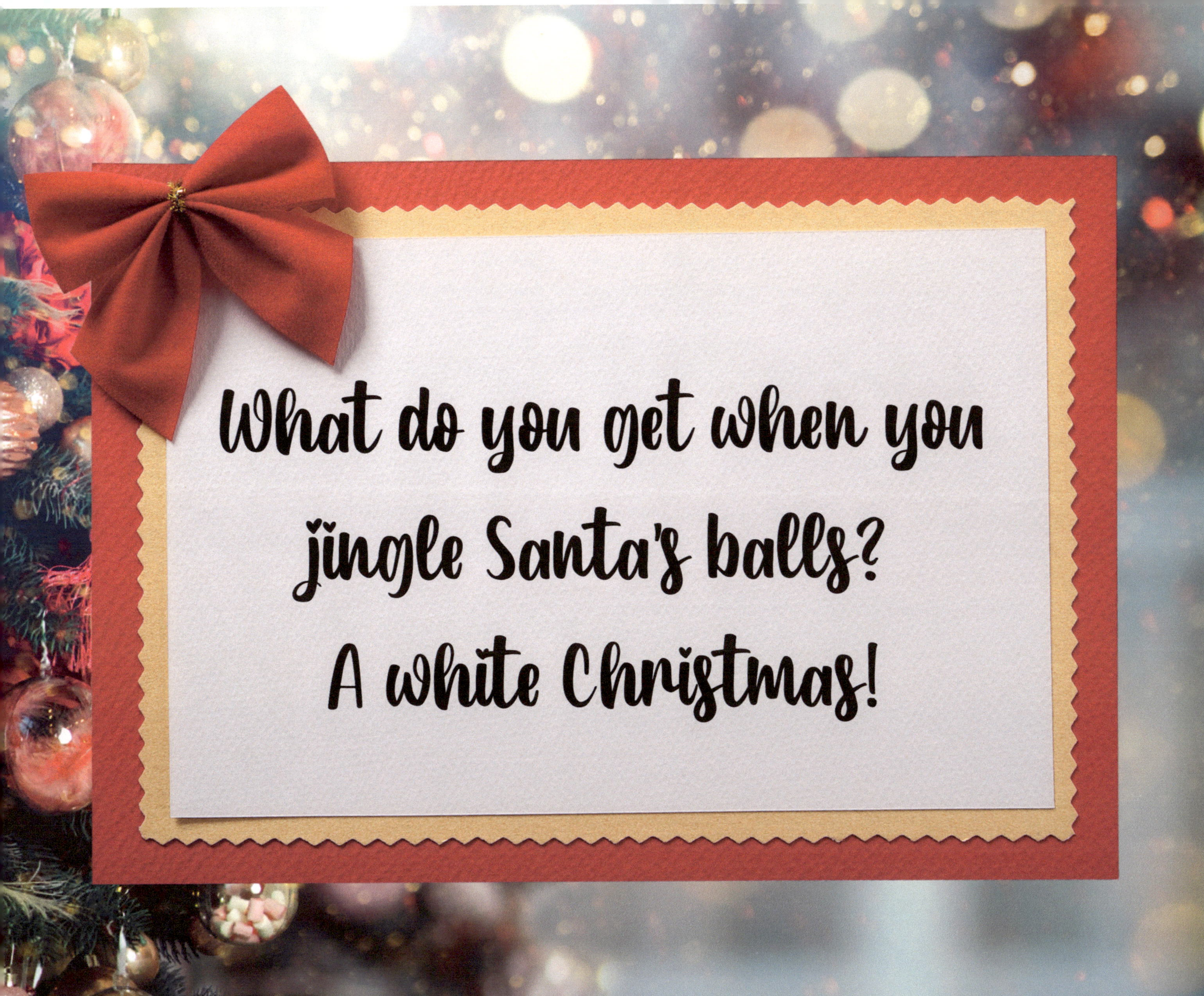
What do you get when you
jingle Santa's balls?
A white Christmas!

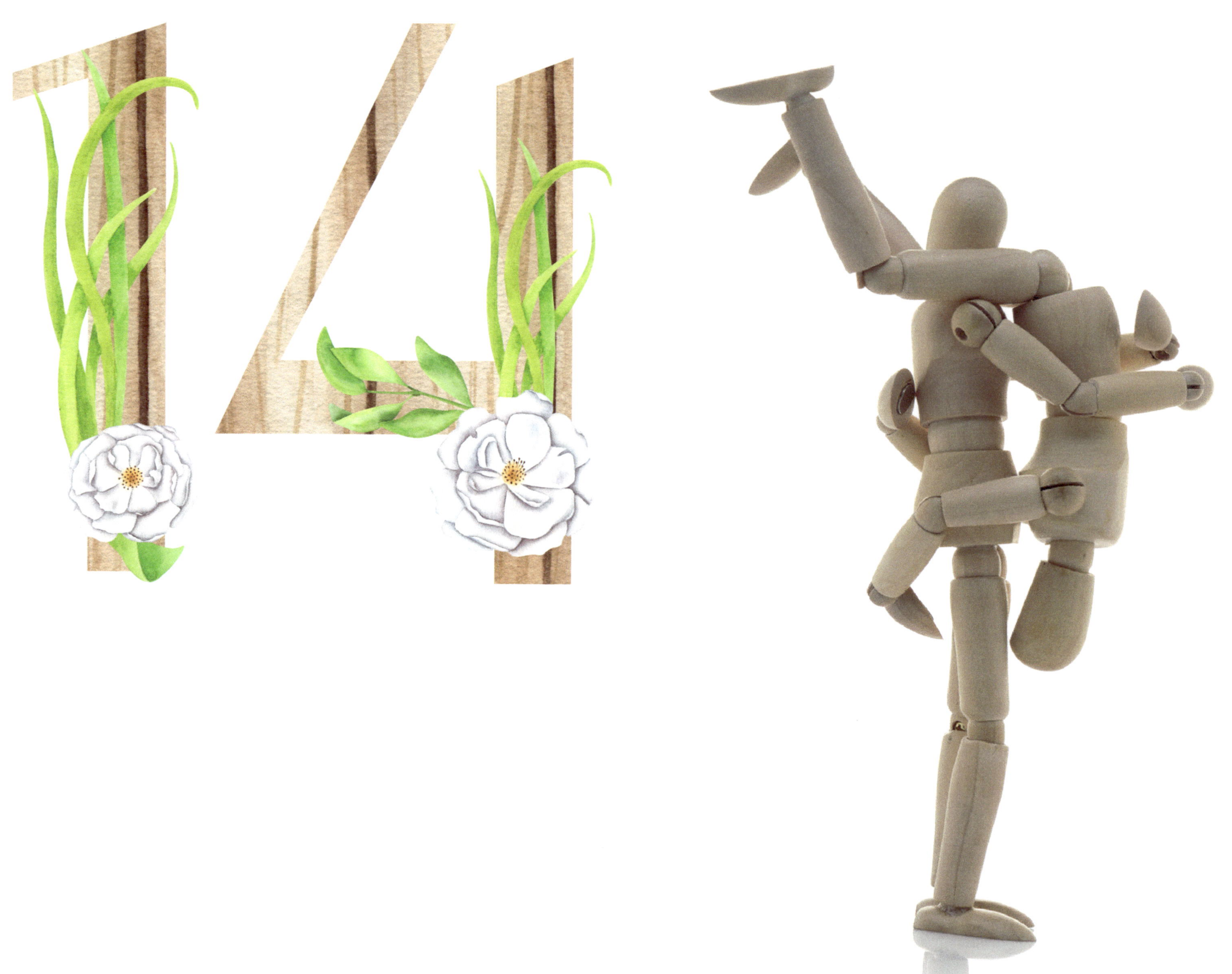
14

A man and a woman started to have sex in the middle of a dark forest. After about 15 minutes, the man finally gets up and says, "Damn, I wish I had a flashlight!" The woman says, "Me too, you've been eating the wrong bush for the past ten minutes!"

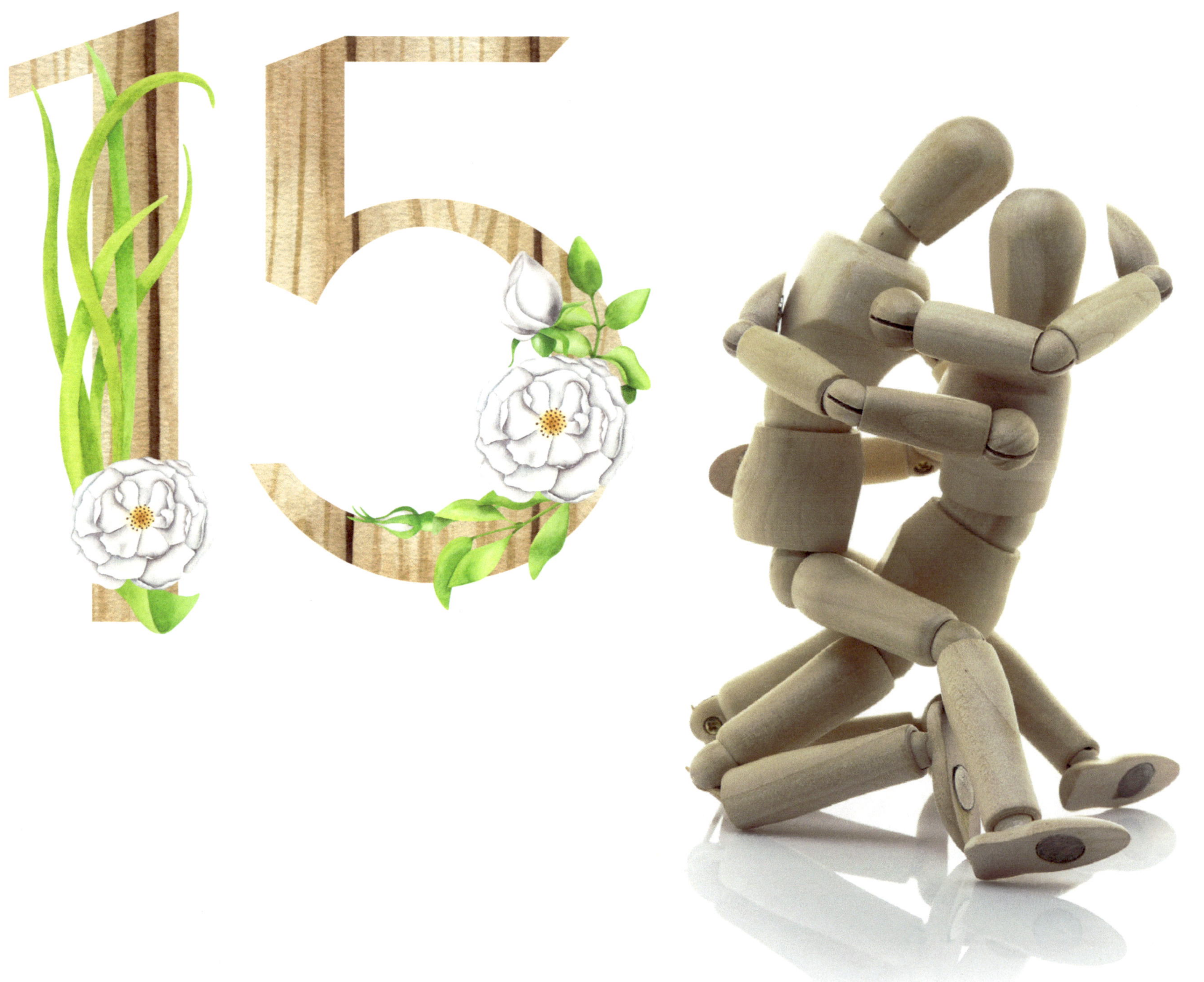
15

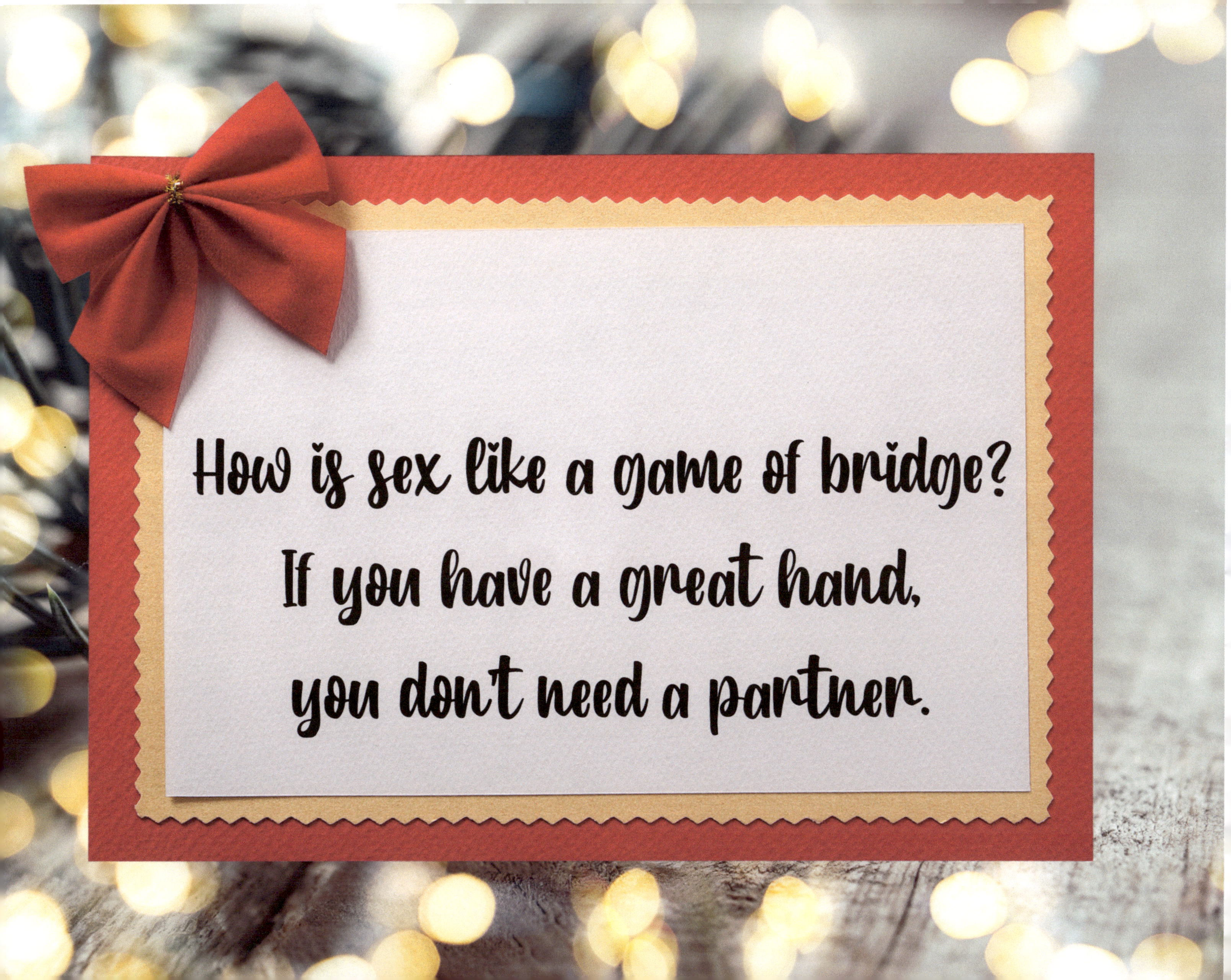
How is sex like a game of bridge?
If you have a great hand,
you don't need a partner.

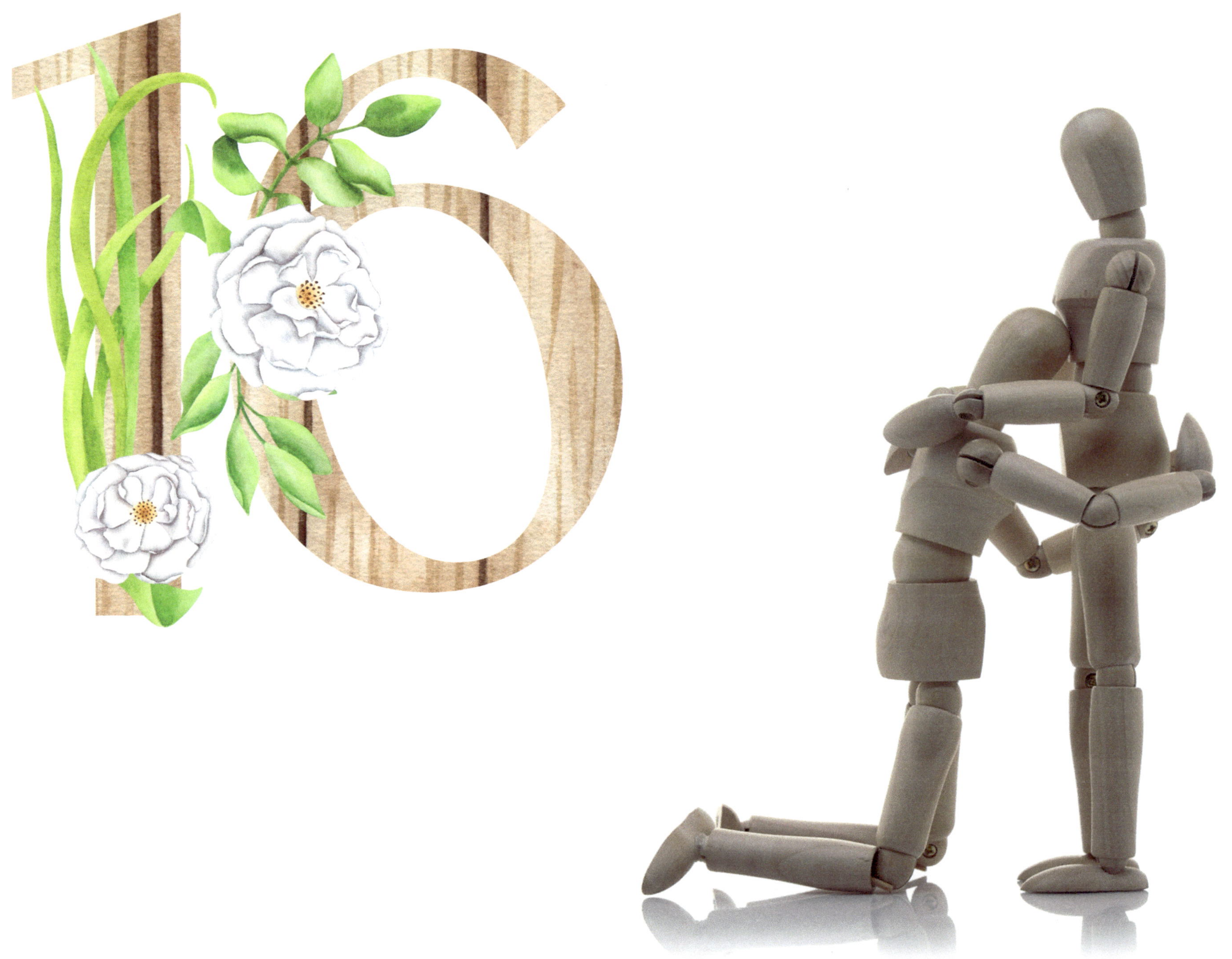
16

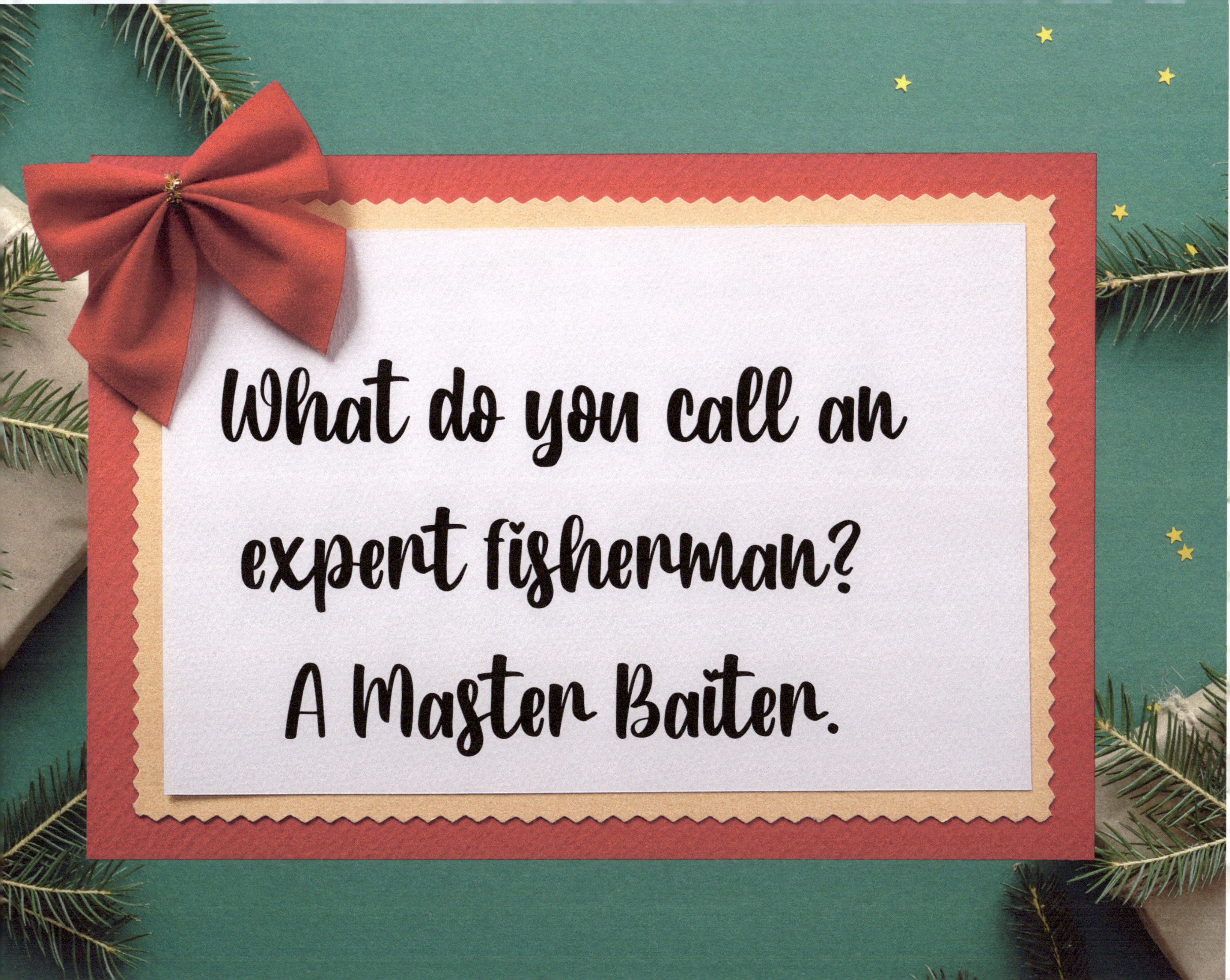
What do you call an
expert fisherman?
A Master Baiter.

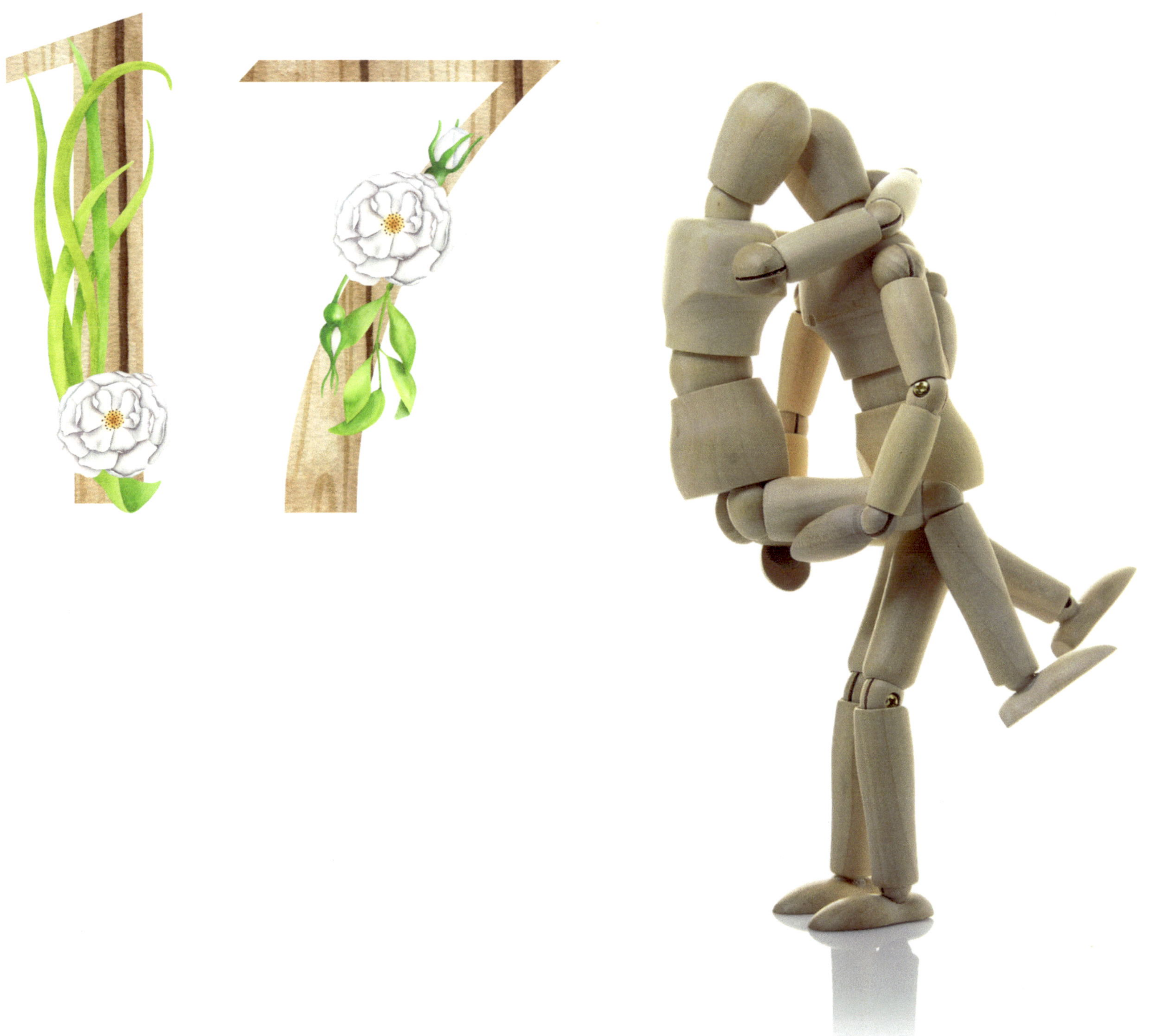
17

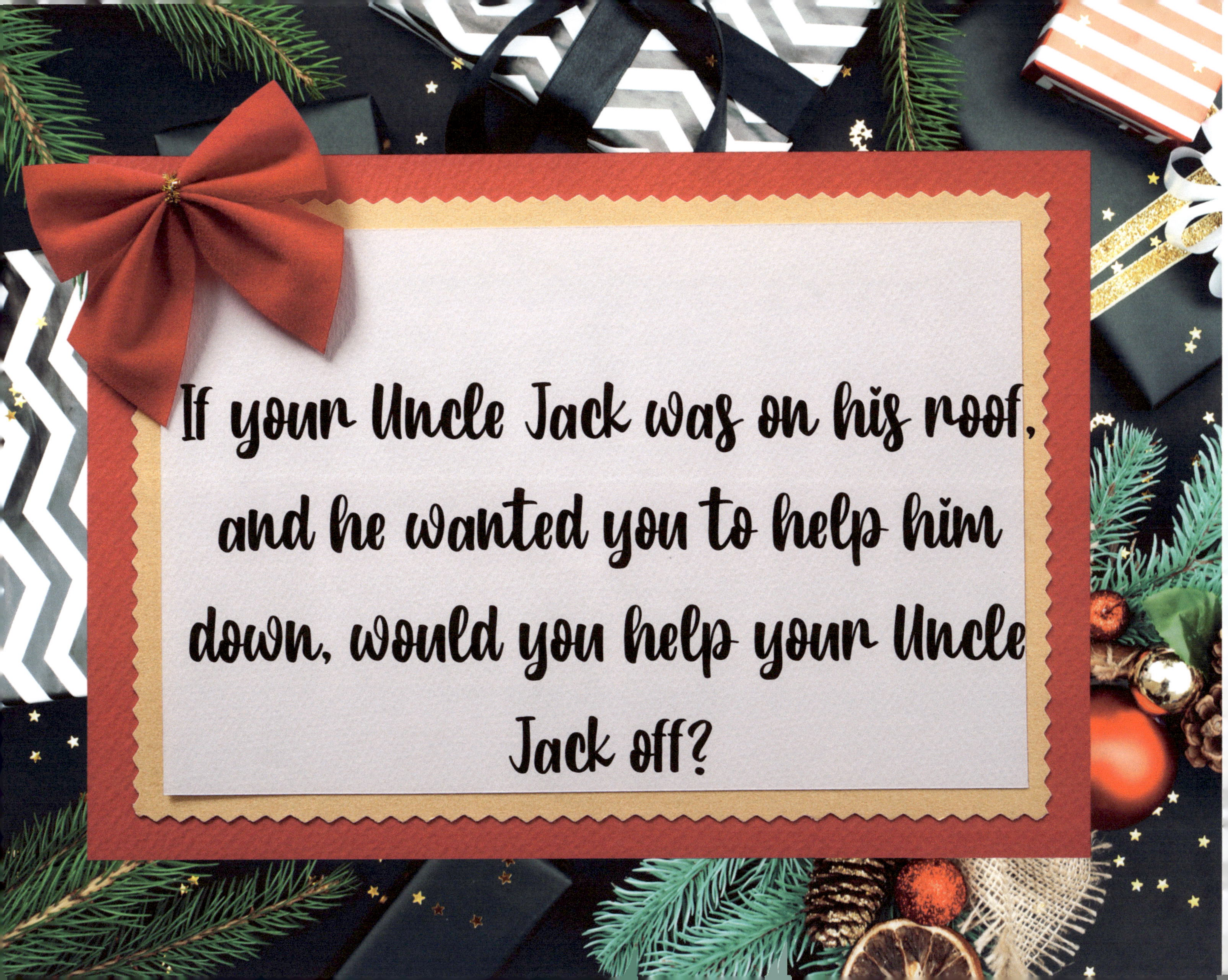
If your Uncle Jack was on his roof,
and he wanted you to help him
down, would you help your Uncle
Jack off?

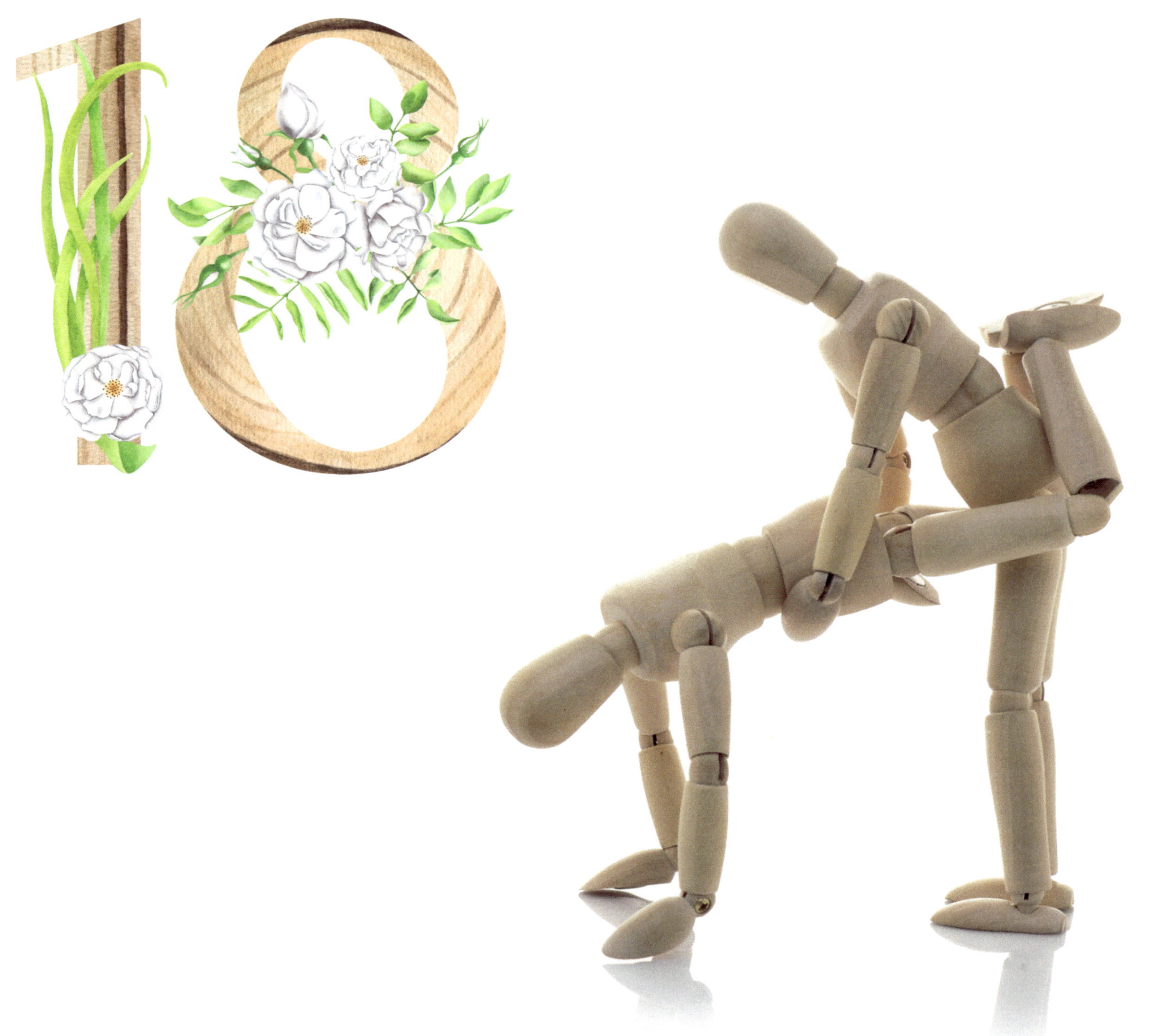
18

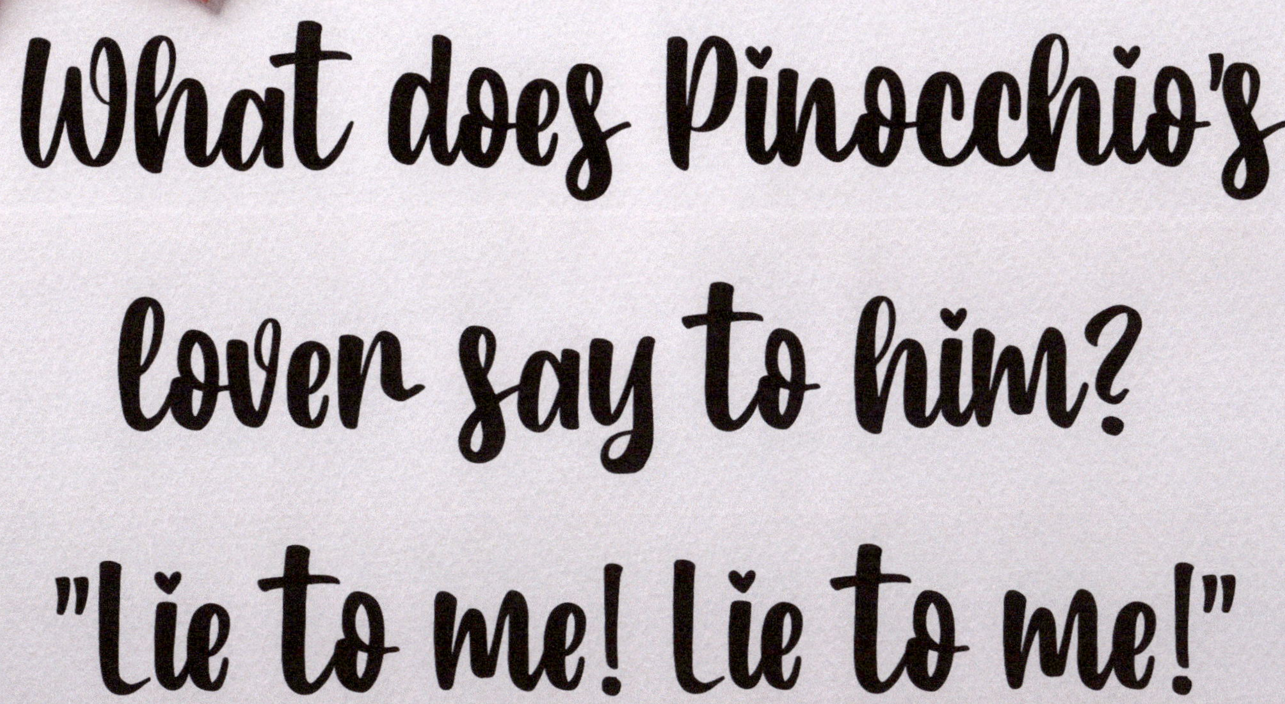
What does Pinocchio's
lover say to him?
"Lie to me! Lie to me!"

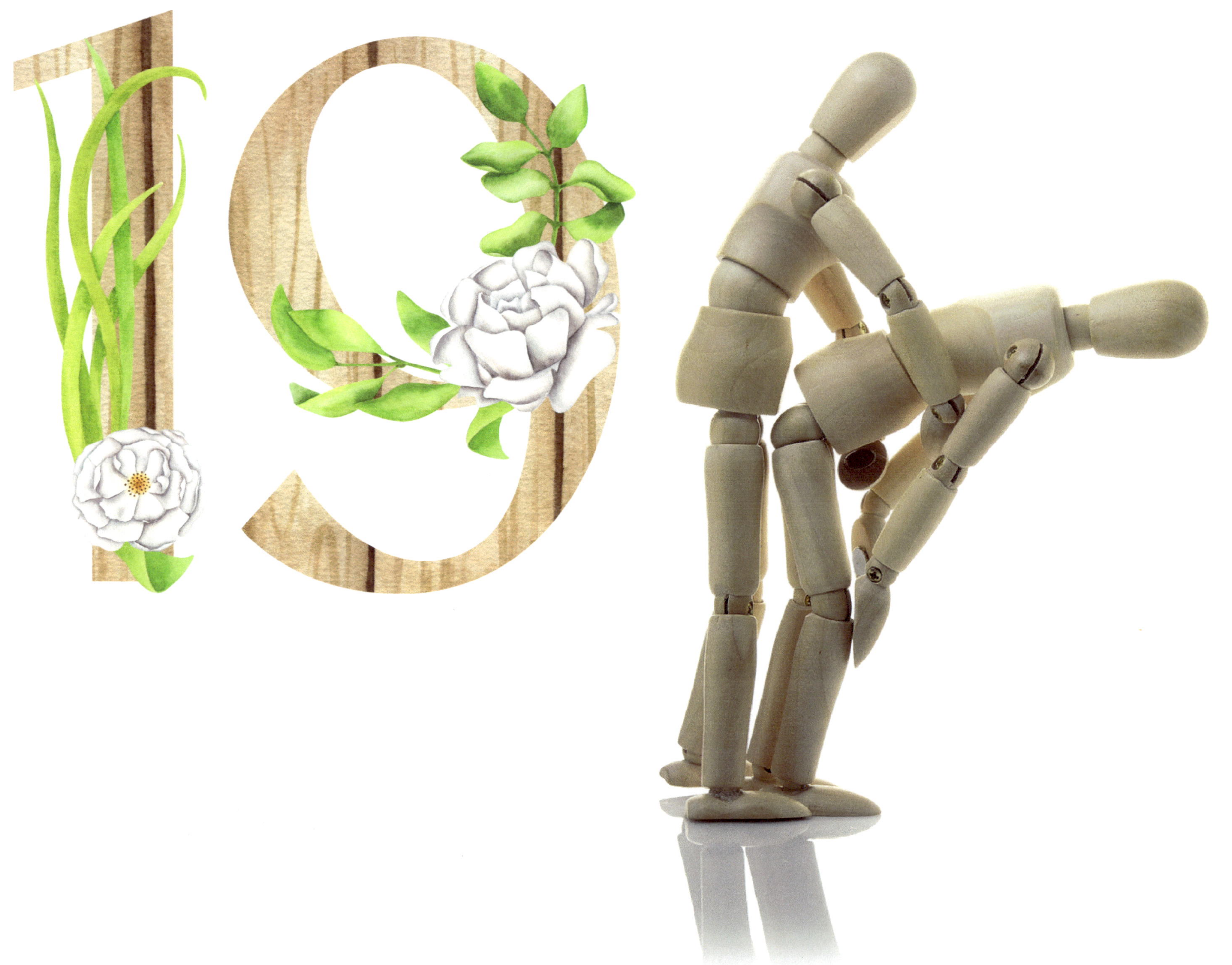
19

A guy is sitting at the doctor's office. The doctor walks in and says, "I have some bad news. I'm afraid you're going to have to stop masturbating."

"I don't understand, why," the patient says.

"Why?"

"Because," the doctor says. "I'm trying to examine you."

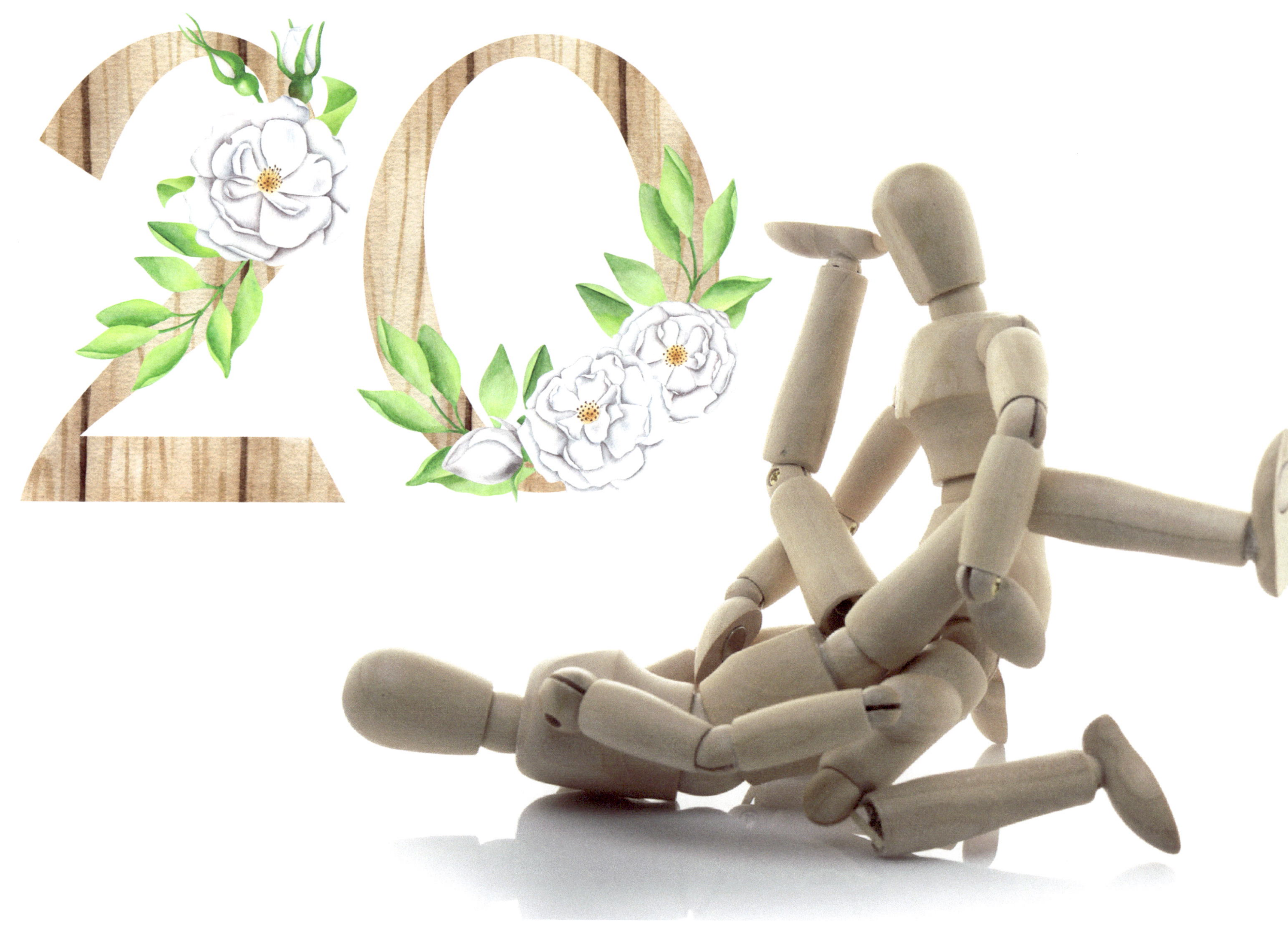
20

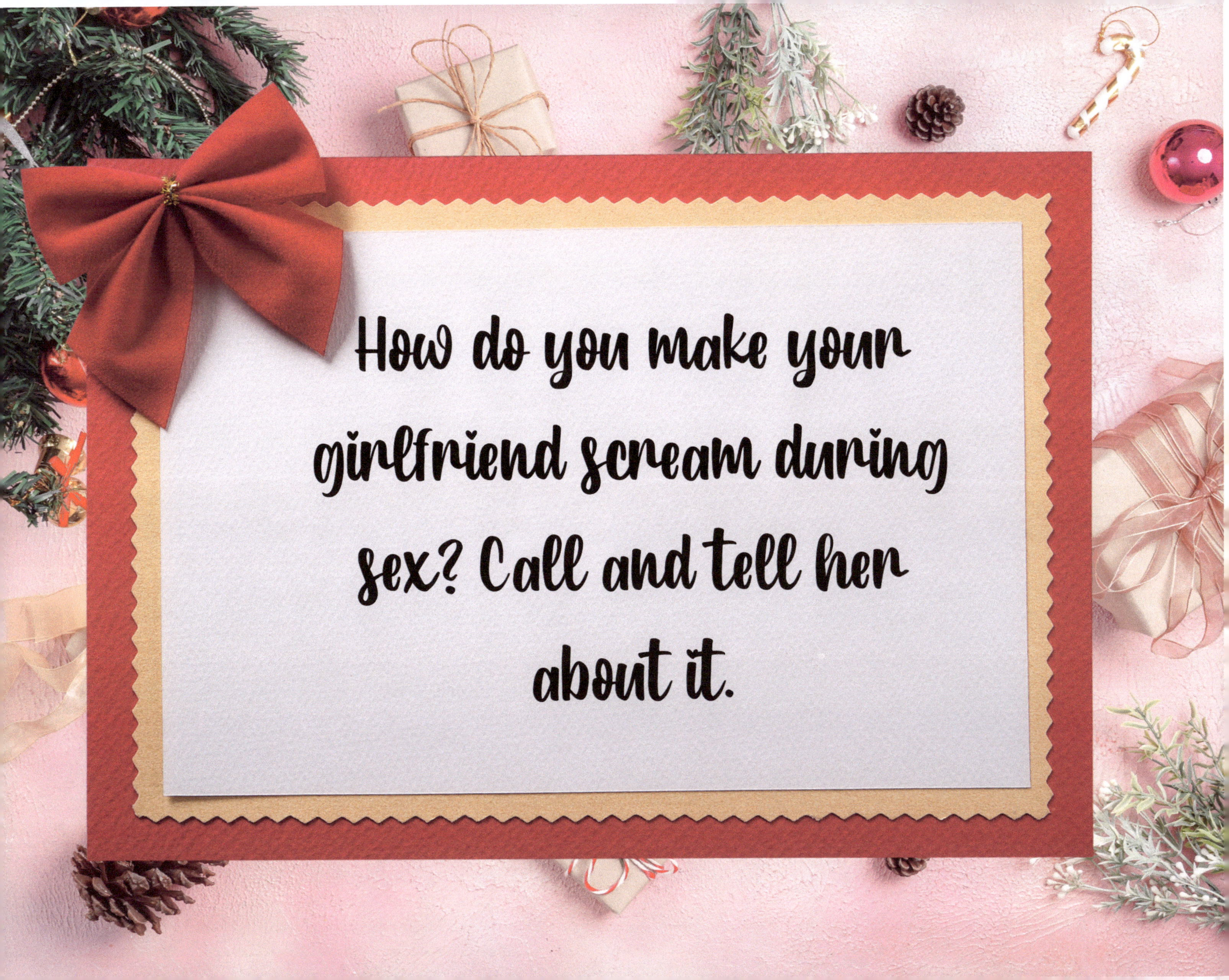
How do you make your
girlfriend scream during
sex? Call and tell her
about it.

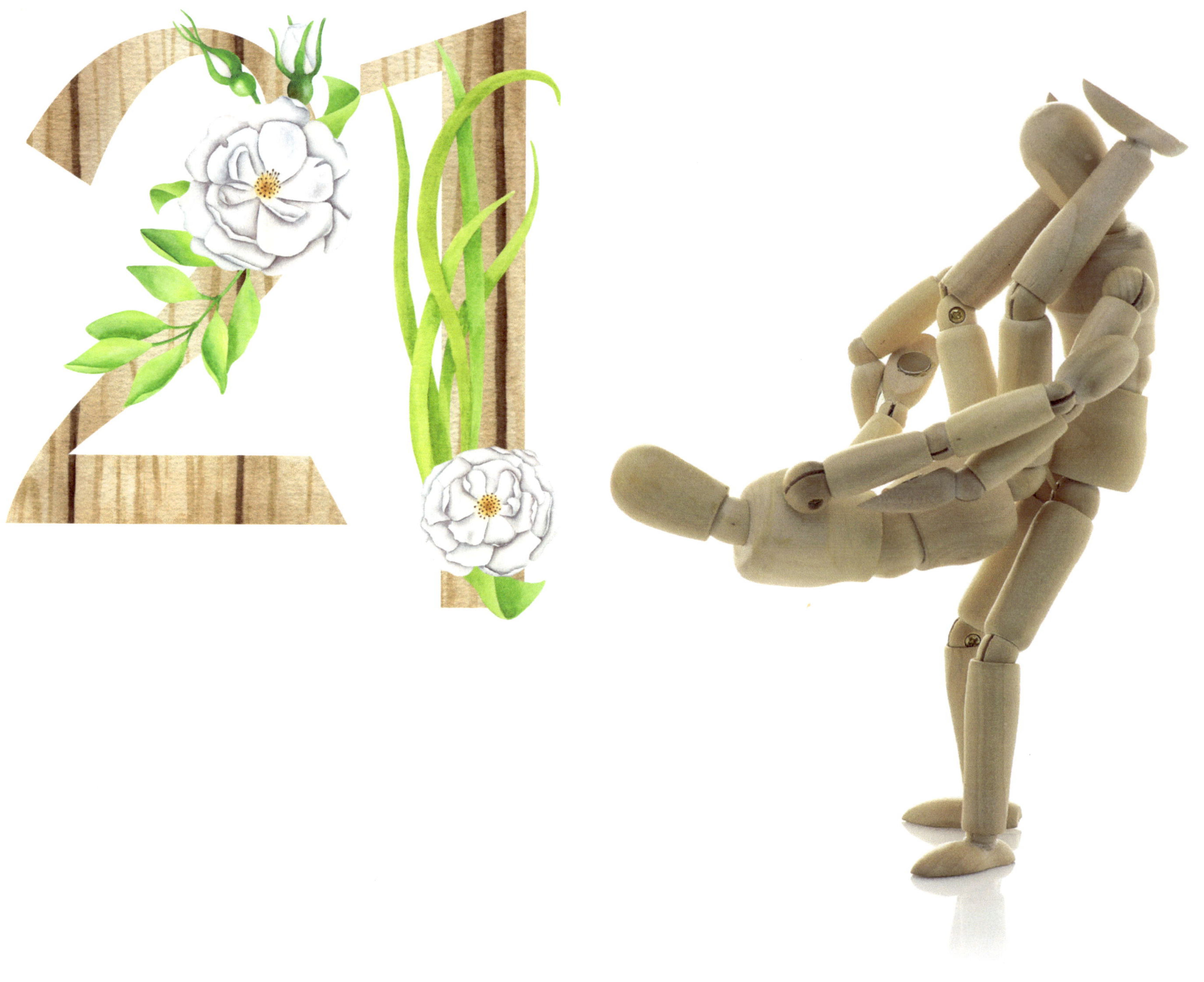
21

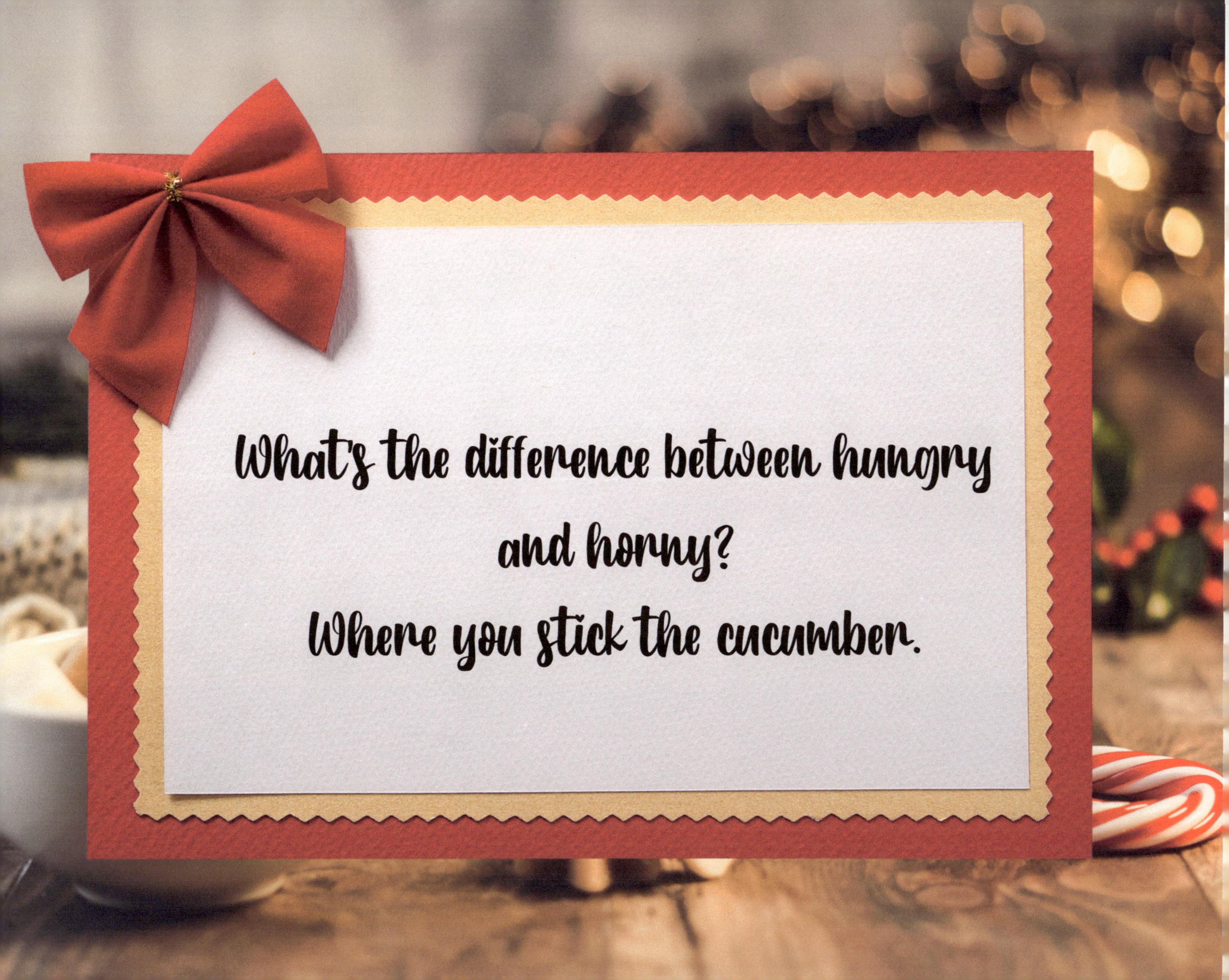
What's the difference between hungry
and horny?
Where you stick the cucumber.

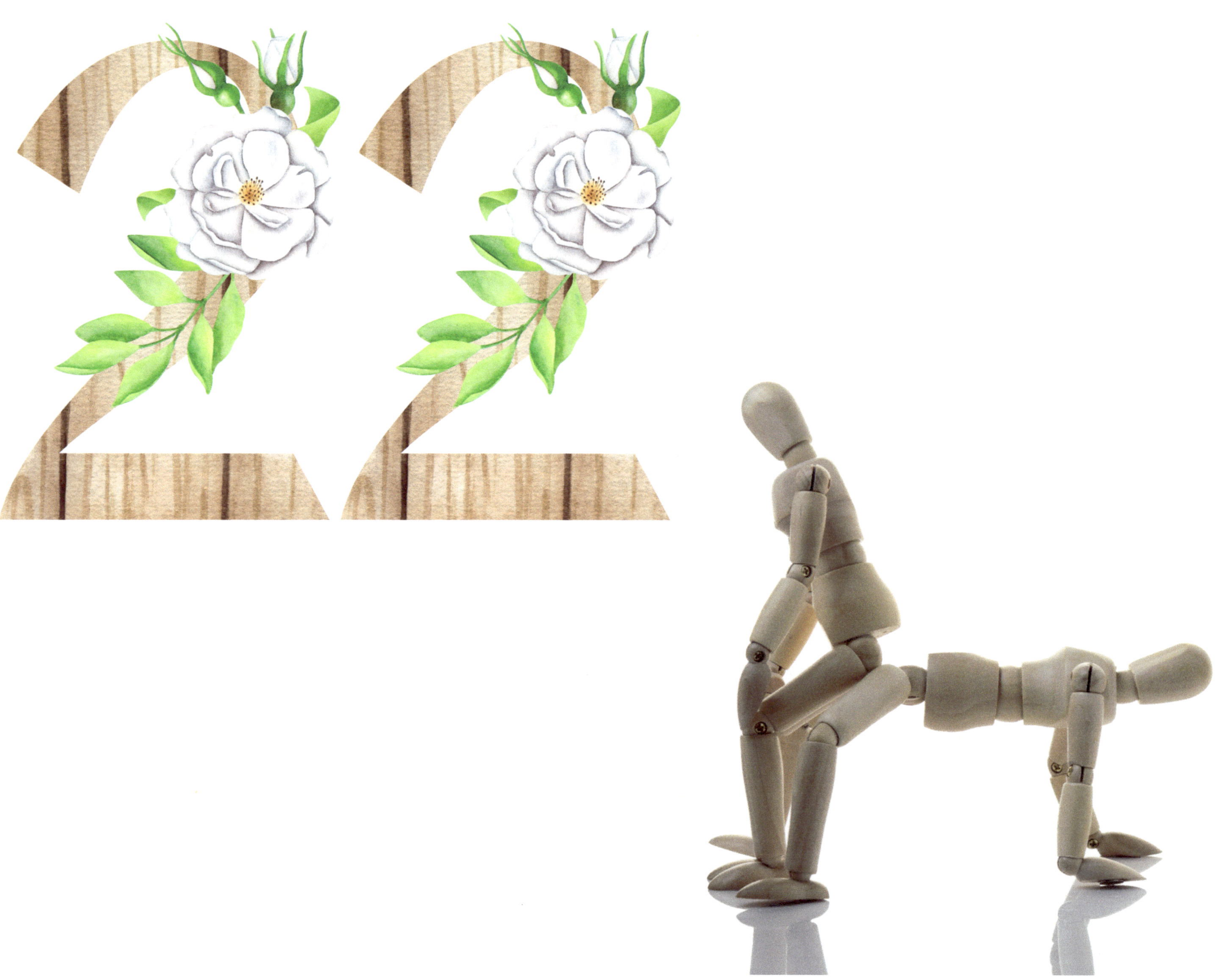
22

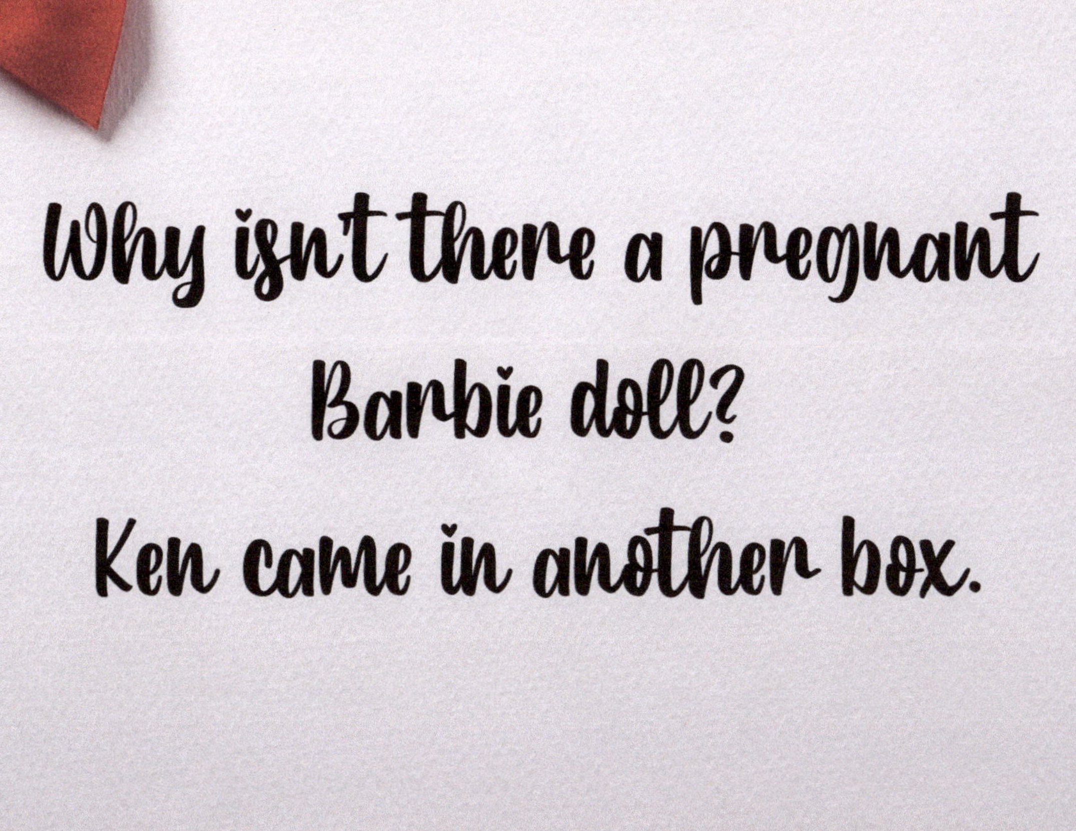
Why isn't there a pregnant
Barbie doll?
Ken came in another box.

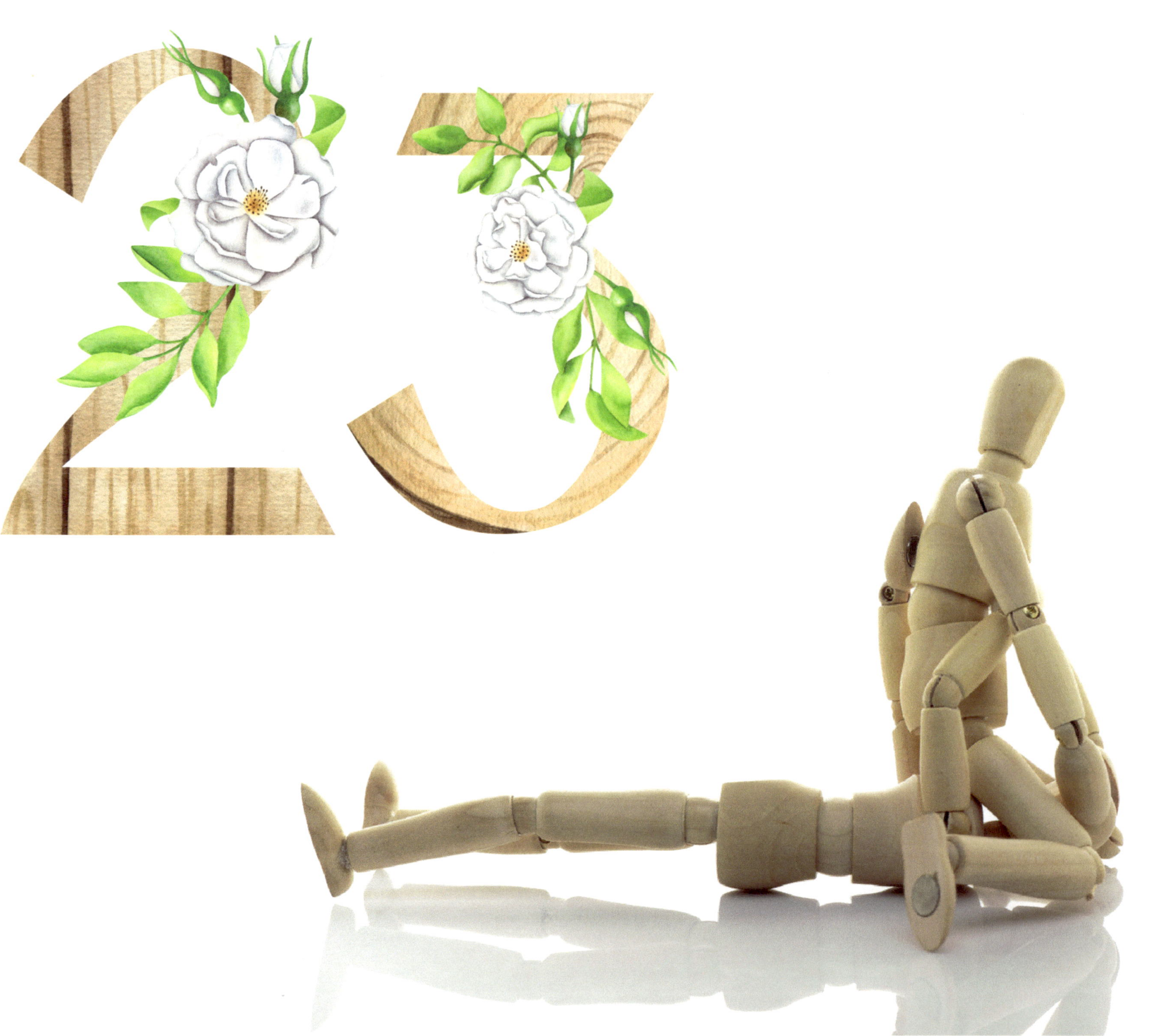
23

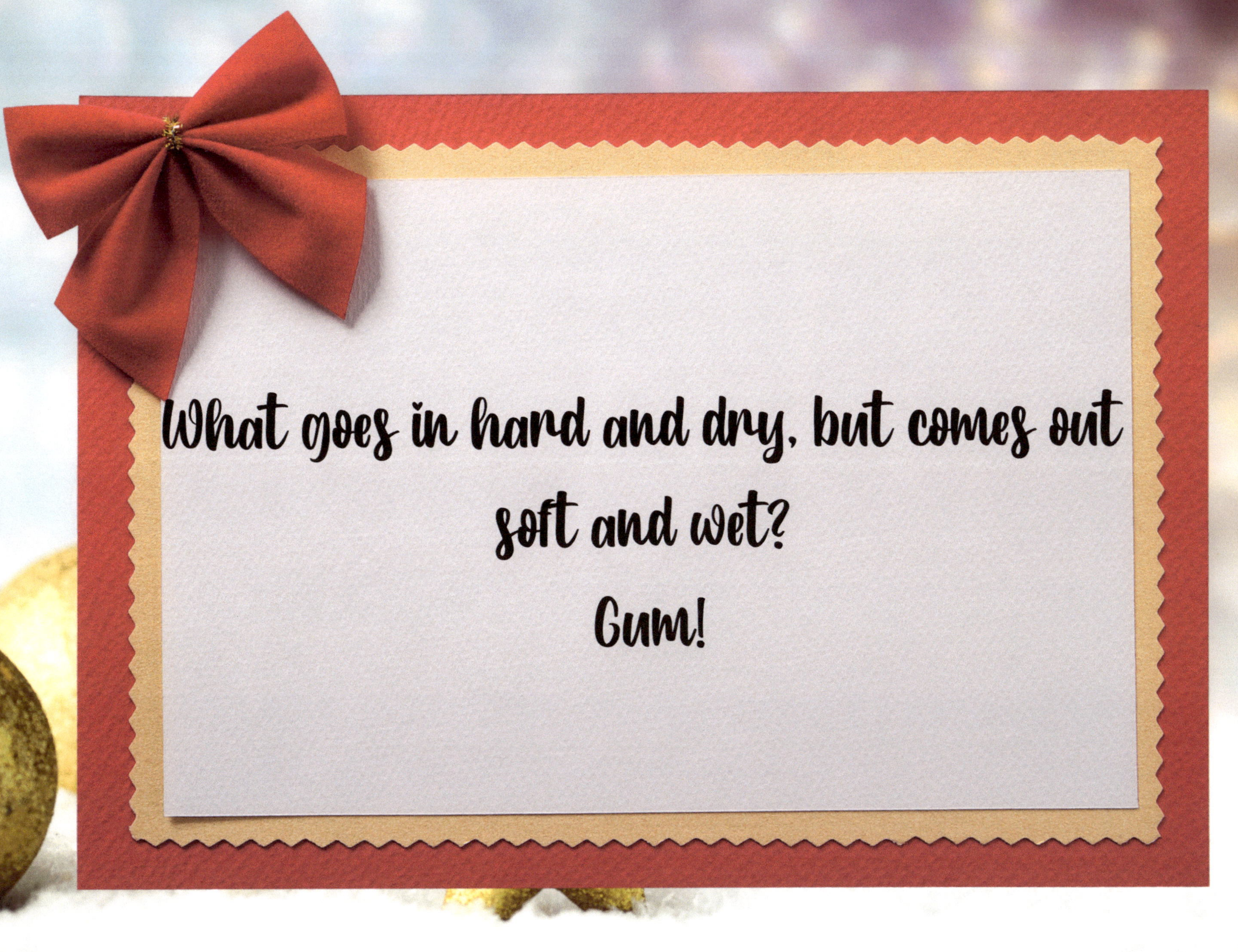
What goes in hard and dry, but comes out soft and wet?
Gum!

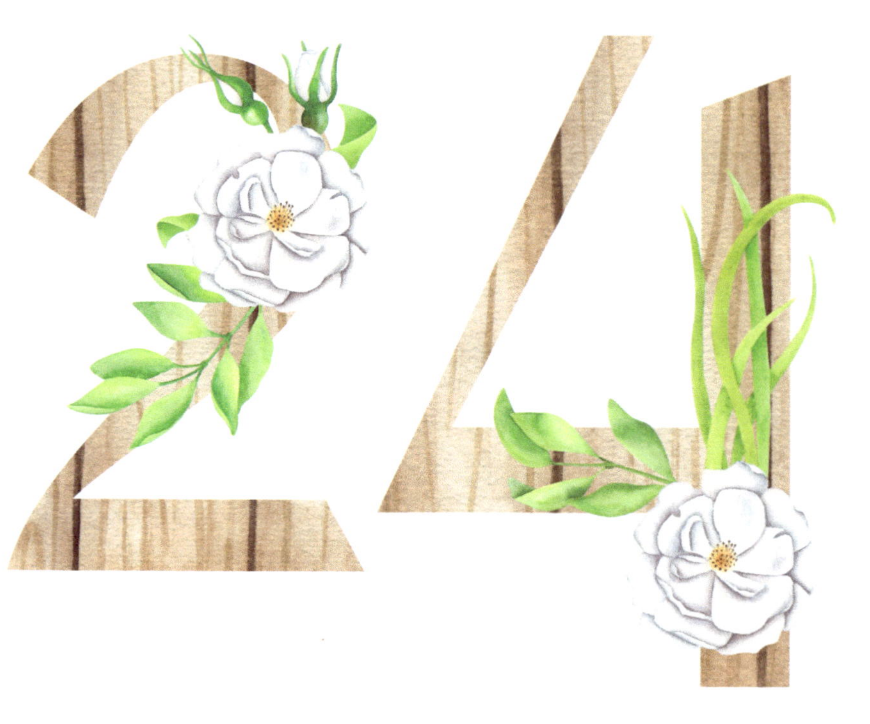
24

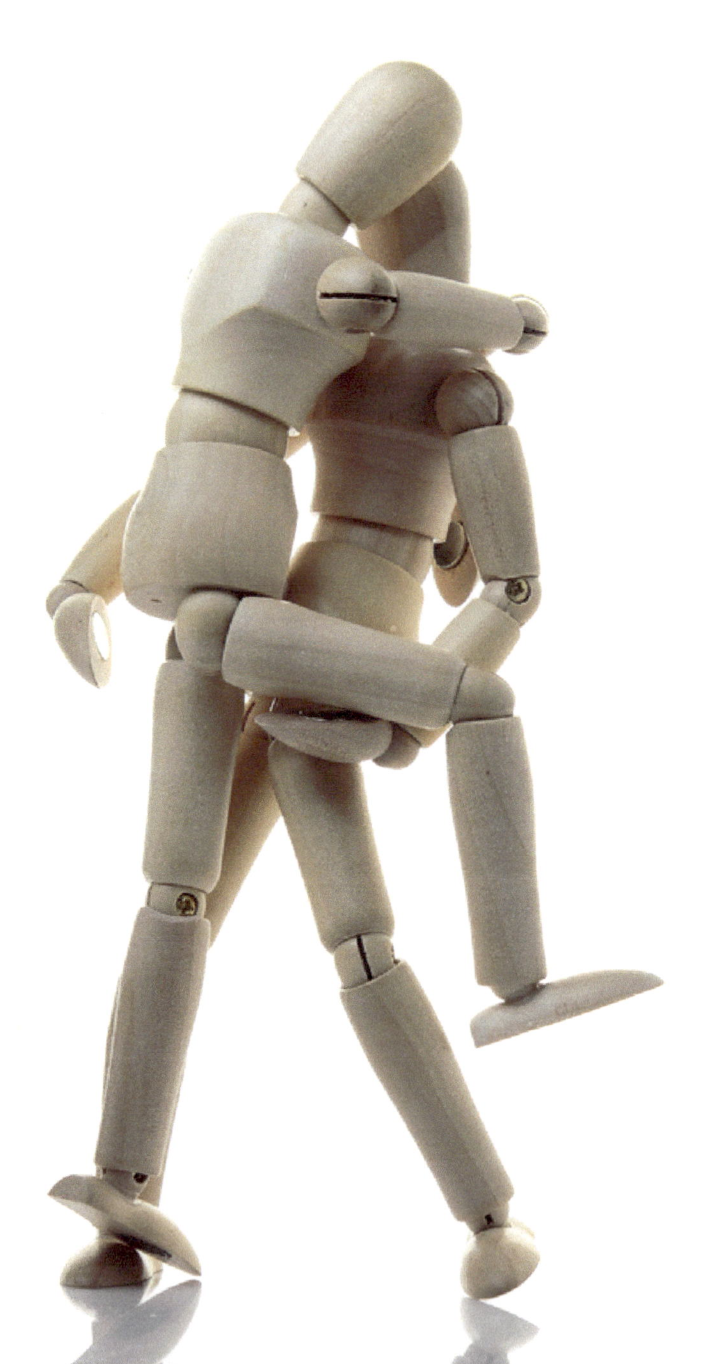

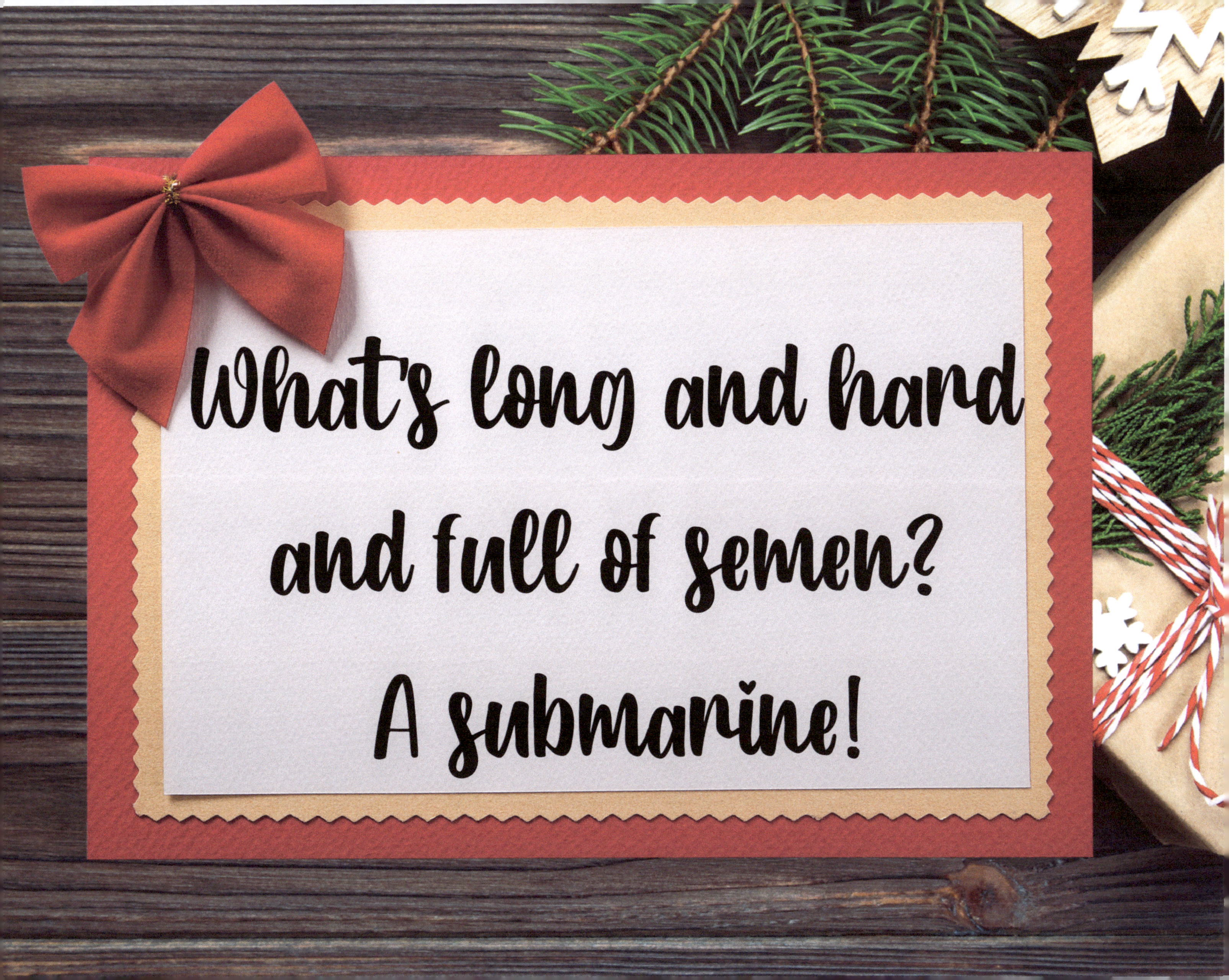
What's long and hard
and full of semen?
A submarine!

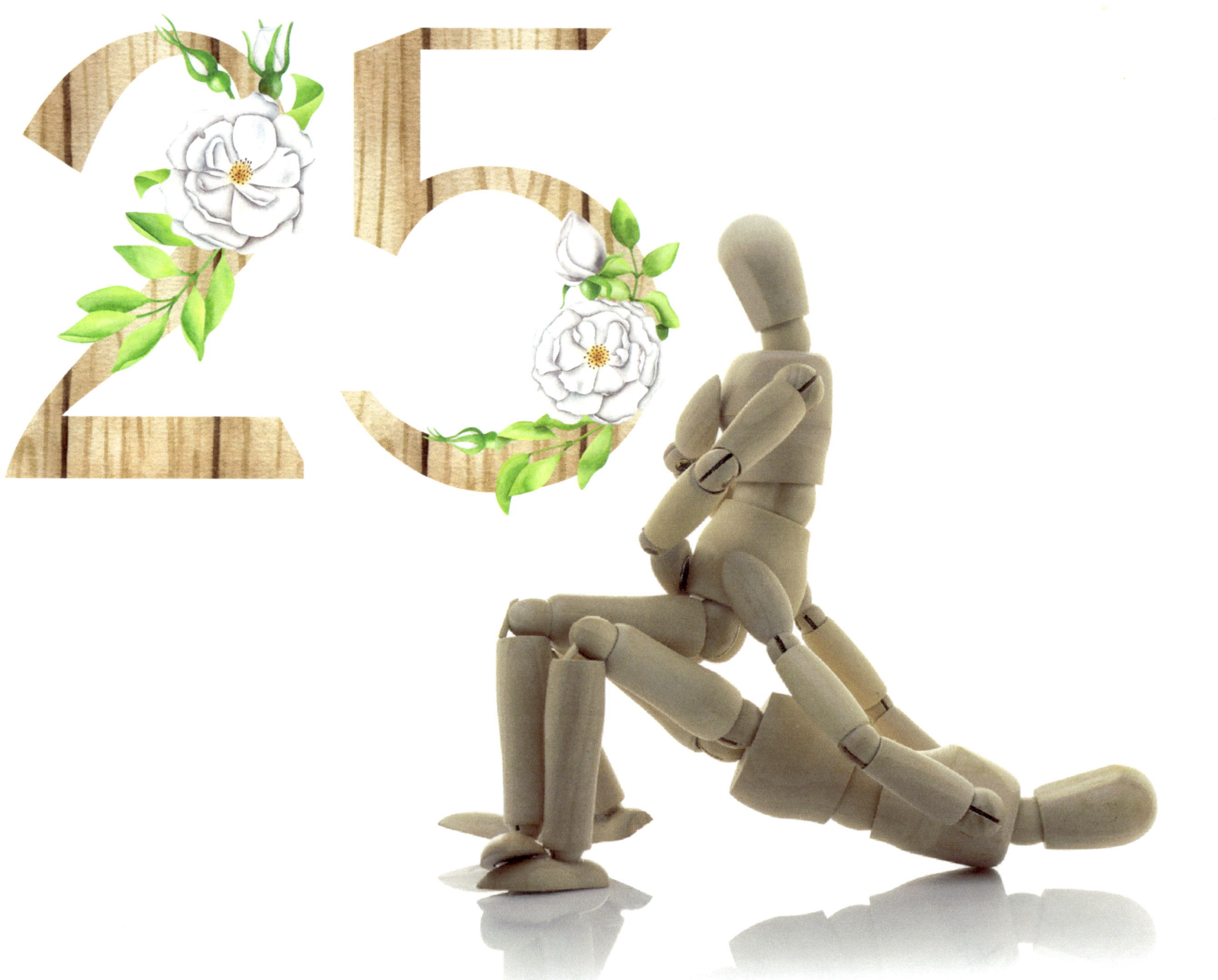
25

www.ingramcontent.com/pod-product-compliance
Lightning Source LLC
Chambersburg PA
CBHW042028050726
47599CB00005B/838